50 Jamaican Patties and Turnovers Recipes for Home

By: Kelly Johnson

Table of Contents

- Traditional Beef Jamaican Patties
- Spicy Jerk Chicken Turnovers
- Curry Vegetable Patties
- Ackee and Saltfish Turnovers
- Vegan Lentil Patties
- Shrimp and Callaloo Turnovers
- Cheesy Spinach Patties
- Sweet Potato and Black Bean Turnovers
- Jamaican Curry Goat Patties
- Tuna and Corn Turnovers
- BBQ Jackfruit Patties
- Jerk Tofu Turnovers
- Beef and Cheese Patties
- Jerk Pork Turnovers
- Coconut Curry Vegetable Patties
- Lobster and Shrimp Turnovers
- Plantain and Black Bean Patties
- Callaloo and Corn Turnovers
- Spicy Chicken Patties
- Saltfish and Okra Turnovers
- Vegan Chickpea Patties
- Mango Curry Chicken Turnovers
- Jamaican Pumpkin Patties
- Escovitch Fish Turnovers
- Curry Chickpea Patties
- Ackee and Callaloo Turnovers
- Spicy Beef Patties
- Jerk Seitan Turnovers
- Sweet Potato and Chickpea Patties
- Tofu and Vegetable Turnovers
- Curried Lamb Patties
- Callaloo and Crab Turnovers
- Pineapple Teriyaki Chicken Patties
- Saltfish and Potato Turnovers
- Vegan BBQ Jackfruit Patties

- Ackee and Ackee Turnovers
- Spicy Shrimp Patties
- Jerk Eggplant Turnovers
- Corned Beef and Cheese Patties
- Coconut Curry Shrimp Turnovers
- Callaloo and Sweet Potato Patties
- Curry Beef Turnovers
- Jamaican Ackee Patties
- Saltfish and Pumpkin Turnovers
- Spicy Lentil Patties
- Jerk Turkey Turnovers
- Plantain and Black Bean Patties
- Callaloo and Sweet Pepper Turnovers
- Vegan Mushroom Patties
- Tamarind BBQ Chicken Turnovers

Traditional Beef Jamaican Patties

Ingredients:

For the pastry:

- 3 cups all-purpose flour
- 1 teaspoon turmeric (for color)
- 1 teaspoon salt
- 1 cup cold vegan butter or vegetable shortening
- 1/2 cup ice water

For the filling:

- 1 tablespoon vegetable oil
- 1 onion, finely chopped
- 2 cloves garlic, minced
- 1 pound ground beef substitute (such as textured vegetable protein or plant-based ground beef)
- 2 teaspoons Jamaican curry powder
- 1 teaspoon dried thyme
- 1 teaspoon paprika
- 1 teaspoon allspice
- Salt and pepper to taste
- 1/4 cup vegetable broth
- Optional: Scotch bonnet pepper or hot sauce to taste (for extra heat)

Instructions:

To make the pastry, sift the flour, turmeric, and salt together in a large mixing bowl. Cut the cold vegan butter or shortening into small cubes and add them to the flour mixture.

Use your fingers or a pastry cutter to rub the butter into the flour until the mixture resembles coarse crumbs.

Gradually add the ice water, a little at a time, mixing until a dough forms. Be careful not to overwork the dough. Shape the dough into a ball, wrap it in plastic wrap, and refrigerate for at least 30 minutes.

While the dough is chilling, prepare the filling. Heat the vegetable oil in a skillet over medium heat. Add the chopped onion and garlic and cook until softened, about 2-3 minutes.

Add the ground beef substitute to the skillet and cook, breaking it up with a spoon, until browned and cooked through.

Stir in the Jamaican curry powder, dried thyme, paprika, allspice, salt, and pepper. Cook for another 2-3 minutes to toast the spices.

Pour in the vegetable broth and simmer for 5-7 minutes, or until the mixture has thickened slightly. Taste and adjust seasoning as needed. If using Scotch bonnet pepper or hot sauce, add it at this stage.

Preheat the oven to 375°F (190°C). Line a baking sheet with parchment paper.

Roll out the chilled dough on a lightly floured surface to about 1/8 inch thickness. Use a round cutter or a small bowl to cut out circles, approximately 5-6 inches in diameter.

Place a spoonful of the beef filling in the center of each pastry circle. Fold the dough over the filling to form a half-moon shape and crimp the edges with a fork to seal.

Place the assembled patties on the prepared baking sheet. Bake in the preheated oven for 25-30 minutes, or until the pastry is golden brown and cooked through.

Allow the patties to cool slightly before serving. Enjoy these traditional Jamaican beef patties warm or at room temperature.

Spicy Jerk Chicken Turnovers
Ingredients:

For the pastry:

- 3 cups all-purpose flour
- 1 teaspoon salt
- 1 cup cold vegan butter or vegetable shortening
- 1/2 cup ice water

For the filling:

- 2 cups cooked shredded chicken (you can use leftover cooked chicken or rotisserie chicken)
- 2 tablespoons Jamaican jerk seasoning
- 1 tablespoon vegetable oil
- 1 onion, finely chopped
- 2 cloves garlic, minced
- 1 bell pepper, finely chopped
- 1 teaspoon dried thyme
- 1 teaspoon paprika
- 1/2 teaspoon cayenne pepper (adjust to taste)
- Salt and pepper to taste
- 1/4 cup chicken broth or water
- Optional: chopped scallions or cilantro for garnish

Instructions:

Preheat the oven to 375°F (190°C). Line a baking sheet with parchment paper.
To make the pastry, sift the flour and salt together in a large mixing bowl. Cut the cold vegan butter or shortening into small cubes and add them to the flour mixture.
Use your fingers or a pastry cutter to rub the butter into the flour until the mixture resembles coarse crumbs.
Gradually add the ice water, a little at a time, mixing until a dough forms. Be careful not to overwork the dough. Shape the dough into a ball, wrap it in plastic wrap, and refrigerate for at least 30 minutes.

While the dough is chilling, prepare the filling. In a mixing bowl, combine the cooked shredded chicken with Jamaican jerk seasoning. Toss until the chicken is evenly coated. Set aside.

Heat the vegetable oil in a skillet over medium heat. Add the chopped onion, garlic, and bell pepper. Cook until softened, about 3-4 minutes.

Add the seasoned shredded chicken to the skillet. Stir in the dried thyme, paprika, cayenne pepper, salt, and pepper. Cook for another 2-3 minutes to allow the flavors to meld together.

Pour in the chicken broth or water and simmer for 5-7 minutes, or until the mixture has thickened slightly. Taste and adjust seasoning as needed.

Remove the chilled dough from the refrigerator. Roll it out on a lightly floured surface to about 1/8 inch thickness. Use a round cutter or a small bowl to cut out circles, approximately 5-6 inches in diameter.

Place a spoonful of the chicken filling in the center of each pastry circle. Fold the dough over the filling to form a half-moon shape and crimp the edges with a fork to seal.

Place the assembled turnovers on the prepared baking sheet. Bake in the preheated oven for 25-30 minutes, or until the pastry is golden brown and cooked through.

Garnish the spicy jerk chicken turnovers with chopped scallions or cilantro before serving. Enjoy them warm as a delicious snack or meal!

Curry Vegetable Patties

Ingredients:

For the pastry:

- 3 cups all-purpose flour
- 1 teaspoon salt
- 1 cup cold vegan butter or vegetable shortening
- 1/2 cup ice water

For the filling:

- 2 tablespoons vegetable oil
- 1 onion, finely chopped
- 2 cloves garlic, minced
- 2 carrots, diced
- 1 medium potato, diced
- 1 cup cauliflower florets, chopped
- 1 cup broccoli florets, chopped
- 2 teaspoons curry powder
- 1 teaspoon ground cumin
- 1/2 teaspoon turmeric powder
- Salt and pepper to taste
- 1/4 cup vegetable broth or water
- Optional: chopped cilantro or parsley for garnish

Instructions:

Preheat the oven to 375°F (190°C). Line a baking sheet with parchment paper.
To make the pastry, sift the flour and salt together in a large mixing bowl. Cut the cold vegan butter or shortening into small cubes and add them to the flour mixture.
Use your fingers or a pastry cutter to rub the butter into the flour until the mixture resembles coarse crumbs.
Gradually add the ice water, a little at a time, mixing until a dough forms. Be careful not to overwork the dough. Shape the dough into a ball, wrap it in plastic wrap, and refrigerate for at least 30 minutes.

While the dough is chilling, prepare the filling. Heat the vegetable oil in a skillet over medium heat. Add the chopped onion and garlic. Cook until softened, about 2-3 minutes.

Add the diced carrots and potato to the skillet. Cook for 5-7 minutes, or until slightly softened.

Stir in the cauliflower and broccoli florets. Cook for another 3-4 minutes.

Add the curry powder, ground cumin, turmeric powder, salt, and pepper. Stir to coat the vegetables evenly with the spices.

Pour in the vegetable broth or water. Cover the skillet and simmer for 8-10 minutes, or until the vegetables are tender and the liquid has reduced. Remove from heat and let the filling cool slightly.

Remove the chilled dough from the refrigerator. Roll it out on a lightly floured surface to about 1/8 inch thickness. Use a round cutter or a small bowl to cut out circles, approximately 5-6 inches in diameter.

Place a spoonful of the vegetable filling in the center of each pastry circle. Fold the dough over the filling to form a half-moon shape and crimp the edges with a fork to seal.

Place the assembled patties on the prepared baking sheet. Bake in the preheated oven for 25-30 minutes, or until the pastry is golden brown and cooked through.

Garnish the curry vegetable patties with chopped cilantro or parsley before serving. Enjoy them warm as a delightful snack or meal!

Ackee and Saltfish Turnovers

Ingredients:

For the pastry:

- 3 cups all-purpose flour
- 1 teaspoon salt
- 1 cup cold vegan butter or vegetable shortening
- 1/2 cup ice water

For the filling:

- 1 tablespoon vegetable oil
- 1 onion, finely chopped
- 2 cloves garlic, minced
- 1 bell pepper, finely chopped
- 1 can (19 oz) ackee, drained and rinsed
- 1 cup flaked salted cod (saltfish), boiled and shredded
- 2 tomatoes, diced
- 1/2 teaspoon dried thyme
- 1/2 teaspoon paprika
- Salt and pepper to taste
- Optional: Scotch bonnet pepper or hot sauce to taste (for extra heat)
- 1/4 cup vegetable broth or water
- Optional: chopped scallions or parsley for garnish

Instructions:

Preheat the oven to 375°F (190°C). Line a baking sheet with parchment paper.

To make the pastry, sift the flour and salt together in a large mixing bowl. Cut the cold vegan butter or shortening into small cubes and add them to the flour mixture.

Use your fingers or a pastry cutter to rub the butter into the flour until the mixture resembles coarse crumbs.

Gradually add the ice water, a little at a time, mixing until a dough forms. Be careful not to overwork the dough. Shape the dough into a ball, wrap it in plastic wrap, and refrigerate for at least 30 minutes.

While the dough is chilling, prepare the filling. Heat the vegetable oil in a skillet over medium heat. Add the chopped onion and garlic. Cook until softened, about 2-3 minutes.

Add the bell pepper to the skillet. Cook for another 2-3 minutes.

Stir in the drained ackee, shredded saltfish, diced tomatoes, dried thyme, paprika, salt, and pepper. If using Scotch bonnet pepper or hot sauce, add it at this stage.

Pour in the vegetable broth or water. Cover the skillet and simmer for 5-7 minutes, or until the flavors have melded together and the mixture has thickened slightly. Taste and adjust seasoning if needed.

Remove the chilled dough from the refrigerator. Roll it out on a lightly floured surface to about 1/8 inch thickness. Use a round cutter or a small bowl to cut out circles, approximately 5-6 inches in diameter.

Place a spoonful of the ackee and saltfish filling in the center of each pastry circle. Fold the dough over the filling to form a half-moon shape and crimp the edges with a fork to seal.

Place the assembled turnovers on the prepared baking sheet. Bake in the preheated oven for 25-30 minutes, or until the pastry is golden brown and cooked through.

Garnish the ackee and saltfish turnovers with chopped scallions or parsley before serving. Enjoy them warm as a delicious snack or meal!

Vegan Lentil Patties

Ingredients:

For the lentil mixture:

- 1 cup dried green or brown lentils, rinsed and drained
- 2 1/2 cups vegetable broth or water
- 1 tablespoon olive oil
- 1 onion, finely chopped
- 2 cloves garlic, minced
- 1 carrot, grated
- 1 stalk celery, finely chopped
- 1 teaspoon ground cumin
- 1 teaspoon paprika
- 1/2 teaspoon ground coriander
- Salt and pepper to taste
- 1 tablespoon tomato paste
- 1 tablespoon soy sauce or tamari
- 1 tablespoon lemon juice
- 1/4 cup chopped fresh parsley or cilantro
- 1/4 cup breadcrumbs (optional, for binding)
- 1/4 cup flour (for coating)

For frying:

- 2-3 tablespoons vegetable oil

Instructions:

In a medium saucepan, combine the lentils and vegetable broth or water. Bring to a boil, then reduce the heat to low and simmer, covered, for 20-25 minutes, or until the lentils are tender and most of the liquid is absorbed. Drain any excess liquid and set aside.

In a skillet, heat the olive oil over medium heat. Add the chopped onion, garlic, grated carrot, and celery. Cook, stirring occasionally, until the vegetables are softened, about 5-7 minutes.

Add the cooked lentils to the skillet along with the ground cumin, paprika, ground coriander, salt, and pepper. Stir in the tomato paste, soy sauce or tamari, and lemon juice. Cook for another 2-3 minutes to allow the flavors to meld together.

Remove the mixture from heat and let it cool slightly. Once cooled, transfer the mixture to a food processor and pulse until it reaches a coarse, slightly chunky consistency. If the mixture seems too wet, you can add breadcrumbs to help bind it together.

Shape the lentil mixture into patties using your hands. If the mixture is too sticky, you can wet your hands slightly to prevent sticking.

Place the flour on a plate and coat each lentil patty lightly with flour.

In a large skillet, heat the vegetable oil over medium-high heat. Once hot, add the lentil patties to the skillet (you may need to work in batches depending on the size of your skillet). Cook for 3-4 minutes on each side, or until golden brown and crispy.

Once cooked, transfer the lentil patties to a plate lined with paper towels to drain any excess oil.

Serve the vegan lentil patties hot with your favorite dipping sauce or as part of a meal with salad and sides. Enjoy!

Shrimp and Callaloo Turnovers

Ingredients:

For the pastry:

- 3 cups all-purpose flour
- 1 teaspoon salt
- 1 cup cold vegan butter or vegetable shortening
- 1/2 cup ice water

For the filling:

- 1 tablespoon vegetable oil
- 1 onion, finely chopped
- 2 cloves garlic, minced
- 1 bell pepper, finely chopped
- 1 tomato, diced
- 1 cup chopped callaloo (substitute spinach if unavailable)
- 1/2 pound shrimp, peeled and deveined, chopped into small pieces
- 1 teaspoon dried thyme
- 1/2 teaspoon paprika
- Salt and pepper to taste
- 1/4 cup vegetable broth or water
- Optional: Scotch bonnet pepper or hot sauce to taste (for extra heat)
- Optional: chopped scallions or parsley for garnish

Instructions:

Preheat the oven to 375°F (190°C). Line a baking sheet with parchment paper.
To make the pastry, sift the flour and salt together in a large mixing bowl. Cut the cold vegan butter or shortening into small cubes and add them to the flour mixture.
Use your fingers or a pastry cutter to rub the butter into the flour until the mixture resembles coarse crumbs.
Gradually add the ice water, a little at a time, mixing until a dough forms. Be careful not to overwork the dough. Shape the dough into a ball, wrap it in plastic wrap, and refrigerate for at least 30 minutes.

While the dough is chilling, prepare the filling. Heat the vegetable oil in a skillet over medium heat. Add the chopped onion and garlic. Cook until softened, about 2-3 minutes.

Add the bell pepper and tomato to the skillet. Cook for another 2-3 minutes.

Stir in the chopped callaloo and cook until wilted, about 2-3 minutes.

Add the chopped shrimp to the skillet. Season with dried thyme, paprika, salt, and pepper. Cook for 3-4 minutes, or until the shrimp are pink and cooked through.

Pour in the vegetable broth or water. If using Scotch bonnet pepper or hot sauce, add it at this stage. Simmer for 2-3 minutes, then remove from heat and let the filling cool slightly.

Remove the chilled dough from the refrigerator. Roll it out on a lightly floured surface to about 1/8 inch thickness. Use a round cutter or a small bowl to cut out circles, approximately 5-6 inches in diameter.

Place a spoonful of the shrimp and callaloo filling in the center of each pastry circle. Fold the dough over the filling to form a half-moon shape and crimp the edges with a fork to seal.

Place the assembled turnovers on the prepared baking sheet. Bake in the preheated oven for 25-30 minutes, or until the pastry is golden brown and cooked through.

Garnish the shrimp and callaloo turnovers with chopped scallions or parsley before serving. Enjoy them warm as a delicious snack or meal!

Cheesy Spinach Patties

Ingredients:

For the spinach mixture:

- 1 tablespoon olive oil
- 1 onion, finely chopped
- 2 cloves garlic, minced
- 6 cups fresh spinach, washed and chopped
- 1 cup grated vegan cheese (such as vegan cheddar or mozzarella)
- 1/4 cup nutritional yeast (optional, for extra cheesy flavor)
- Salt and pepper to taste
- 1/4 teaspoon nutmeg (optional, for flavor)

For the patties:

- 2 cups mashed potatoes (about 4 medium potatoes, boiled and mashed)
- 1 cup breadcrumbs (plus extra for coating)
- 2 tablespoons flaxseed meal (mixed with 6 tablespoons water, let sit for 5 minutes to form a flax egg)
- 1/4 cup chopped fresh parsley or cilantro
- Vegetable oil, for frying

Instructions:

Heat the olive oil in a large skillet over medium heat. Add the chopped onion and garlic. Cook until softened, about 2-3 minutes.

Add the chopped spinach to the skillet. Cook, stirring occasionally, until the spinach has wilted and any excess liquid has evaporated, about 5-7 minutes.

Remove the skillet from the heat and let the spinach mixture cool slightly. Once cooled, transfer it to a mixing bowl.

To the bowl with the spinach mixture, add the grated vegan cheese, nutritional yeast (if using), salt, pepper, and nutmeg. Stir until well combined.

In a separate large mixing bowl, combine the mashed potatoes, breadcrumbs, flaxseed meal mixture (flax egg), and chopped parsley or cilantro. Mix until well combined.

Add the spinach and cheese mixture to the bowl with the potato mixture. Stir until all the ingredients are evenly distributed.

Shape the mixture into patties using your hands. If the mixture is too sticky, you can wet your hands slightly to prevent sticking.

Place some breadcrumbs on a plate. Coat each spinach patty lightly with breadcrumbs.

Heat vegetable oil in a large skillet over medium heat. Once hot, add the spinach patties to the skillet (you may need to work in batches depending on the size of your skillet). Cook for 3-4 minutes on each side, or until golden brown and crispy.

Once cooked, transfer the cheesy spinach patties to a plate lined with paper towels to drain any excess oil.

Serve the cheesy spinach patties hot with your favorite dipping sauce or as part of a meal with salad and sides. Enjoy!

Sweet Potato and Black Bean Turnovers

Ingredients:

For the pastry:

- 3 cups all-purpose flour
- 1 teaspoon salt
- 1 cup cold vegan butter or vegetable shortening
- 1/2 cup ice water

For the filling:

- 2 medium sweet potatoes, peeled and diced
- 1 tablespoon olive oil
- 1 onion, finely chopped
- 2 cloves garlic, minced
- 1 bell pepper, diced
- 1 can (15 oz) black beans, drained and rinsed
- 1 teaspoon ground cumin
- 1 teaspoon chili powder
- 1/2 teaspoon paprika
- Salt and pepper to taste
- 1/4 cup chopped fresh cilantro
- Optional: lime wedges for serving

Instructions:

Preheat the oven to 375°F (190°C). Line a baking sheet with parchment paper.
To make the pastry, sift the flour and salt together in a large mixing bowl. Cut the cold vegan butter or shortening into small cubes and add them to the flour mixture.
Use your fingers or a pastry cutter to rub the butter into the flour until the mixture resembles coarse crumbs.
Gradually add the ice water, a little at a time, mixing until a dough forms. Be careful not to overwork the dough. Shape the dough into a ball, wrap it in plastic wrap, and refrigerate for at least 30 minutes.

While the dough is chilling, prepare the filling. Place the diced sweet potatoes in a microwave-safe bowl and microwave on high for 5-7 minutes, or until tender. Alternatively, you can boil the sweet potatoes until tender. Mash the cooked sweet potatoes and set aside.

Heat the olive oil in a skillet over medium heat. Add the chopped onion, garlic, and bell pepper. Cook until softened, about 2-3 minutes.

Add the black beans to the skillet, along with the mashed sweet potatoes, ground cumin, chili powder, paprika, salt, and pepper. Stir to combine and cook for another 2-3 minutes. Remove from heat and stir in the chopped cilantro.

Remove the chilled dough from the refrigerator. Roll it out on a lightly floured surface to about 1/8 inch thickness. Use a round cutter or a small bowl to cut out circles, approximately 5-6 inches in diameter.

Place a spoonful of the sweet potato and black bean filling in the center of each pastry circle. Fold the dough over the filling to form a half-moon shape and crimp the edges with a fork to seal.

Place the assembled turnovers on the prepared baking sheet. Bake in the preheated oven for 25-30 minutes, or until the pastry is golden brown and cooked through.

Serve the sweet potato and black bean turnovers hot, optionally with lime wedges on the side for squeezing over the turnovers. Enjoy!

Jamaican Curry Goat Patties

Ingredients:

For the pastry:

- 3 cups all-purpose flour
- 1 teaspoon salt
- 1 cup cold vegan butter or vegetable shortening
- 1/2 cup ice water

For the filling:

- 1 tablespoon vegetable oil
- 1 onion, finely chopped
- 2 cloves garlic, minced
- 1 pound boneless goat meat, diced into small pieces
- 2 tablespoons Jamaican curry powder
- 1 teaspoon dried thyme
- 1 teaspoon paprika
- 1/2 teaspoon ground allspice
- Salt and pepper to taste
- 1 cup vegetable broth or water
- 1 tablespoon tomato paste
- Optional: Scotch bonnet pepper or hot sauce to taste (for extra heat)
- Optional: chopped fresh cilantro or parsley for garnish

Instructions:

Preheat the oven to 375°F (190°C). Line a baking sheet with parchment paper.
To make the pastry, sift the flour and salt together in a large mixing bowl. Cut the cold vegan butter or shortening into small cubes and add them to the flour mixture.
Use your fingers or a pastry cutter to rub the butter into the flour until the mixture resembles coarse crumbs.
Gradually add the ice water, a little at a time, mixing until a dough forms. Be careful not to overwork the dough. Shape the dough into a ball, wrap it in plastic wrap, and refrigerate for at least 30 minutes.

While the dough is chilling, prepare the filling. Heat the vegetable oil in a skillet over medium heat. Add the chopped onion and garlic. Cook until softened, about 2-3 minutes.

Add the diced goat meat to the skillet. Cook until browned on all sides, about 5-7 minutes.

Stir in the Jamaican curry powder, dried thyme, paprika, ground allspice, salt, and pepper. Cook for another 2-3 minutes to toast the spices.

Pour in the vegetable broth or water and tomato paste. If using Scotch bonnet pepper or hot sauce, add it at this stage. Cover the skillet and simmer for 1-1.5 hours, or until the goat meat is tender and cooked through. Stir occasionally and add more liquid if needed.

Once the meat is cooked, remove the skillet from heat and let the filling cool slightly.

Remove the chilled dough from the refrigerator. Roll it out on a lightly floured surface to about 1/8 inch thickness. Use a round cutter or a small bowl to cut out circles, approximately 5-6 inches in diameter.

Place a spoonful of the curry goat filling in the center of each pastry circle. Fold the dough over the filling to form a half-moon shape and crimp the edges with a fork to seal.

Place the assembled patties on the prepared baking sheet. Bake in the preheated oven for 25-30 minutes, or until the pastry is golden brown and cooked through.

Garnish the Jamaican curry goat patties with chopped fresh cilantro or parsley before serving. Enjoy them warm as a delicious snack or meal!

Tuna and Corn Turnovers

Ingredients:

For the pastry:

- 3 cups all-purpose flour
- 1 teaspoon salt
- 1 cup cold vegan butter or vegetable shortening
- 1/2 cup ice water

For the filling:

- 2 tablespoons vegetable oil
- 1 onion, finely chopped
- 2 cloves garlic, minced
- 1 bell pepper, finely chopped
- 1 can (5 oz) tuna, drained
- 1 cup frozen or canned corn kernels, drained
- 1 teaspoon dried thyme
- 1 teaspoon paprika
- Salt and pepper to taste
- 1/4 cup mayonnaise (vegan if desired)
- 1 tablespoon lemon juice
- Optional: chopped fresh parsley or cilantro for garnish

Instructions:

Preheat the oven to 375°F (190°C). Line a baking sheet with parchment paper. To make the pastry, sift the flour and salt together in a large mixing bowl. Cut the cold vegan butter or shortening into small cubes and add them to the flour mixture.

Use your fingers or a pastry cutter to rub the butter into the flour until the mixture resembles coarse crumbs.

Gradually add the ice water, a little at a time, mixing until a dough forms. Be careful not to overwork the dough. Shape the dough into a ball, wrap it in plastic wrap, and refrigerate for at least 30 minutes.

While the dough is chilling, prepare the filling. Heat the vegetable oil in a skillet over medium heat. Add the chopped onion and garlic. Cook until softened, about 2-3 minutes.

Add the chopped bell pepper to the skillet. Cook for another 2-3 minutes.

Stir in the drained tuna and corn kernels. Season with dried thyme, paprika, salt, and pepper. Cook for 3-4 minutes, stirring occasionally.

In a small bowl, mix together the mayonnaise and lemon juice. Pour this mixture over the tuna and corn mixture in the skillet. Stir until everything is well combined. Remove from heat and let the filling cool slightly.

Remove the chilled dough from the refrigerator. Roll it out on a lightly floured surface to about 1/8 inch thickness. Use a round cutter or a small bowl to cut out circles, approximately 5-6 inches in diameter.

Place a spoonful of the tuna and corn filling in the center of each pastry circle. Fold the dough over the filling to form a half-moon shape and crimp the edges with a fork to seal.

Place the assembled turnovers on the prepared baking sheet. Bake in the preheated oven for 25-30 minutes, or until the pastry is golden brown and cooked through.

Garnish the tuna and corn turnovers with chopped fresh parsley or cilantro before serving. Enjoy them warm as a delicious snack or meal!

BBQ Jackfruit Patties

Ingredients:

For the BBQ Jackfruit:

- 2 cans (20 oz each) young green jackfruit in brine, drained and rinsed
- 1 tablespoon vegetable oil
- 1 onion, finely chopped
- 2 cloves garlic, minced
- 1 cup barbecue sauce
- 1/2 cup vegetable broth or water
- 2 tablespoons tomato paste
- 1 tablespoon soy sauce or tamari
- 1 tablespoon apple cider vinegar
- 1 teaspoon smoked paprika
- 1 teaspoon ground cumin
- Salt and pepper to taste

For the patties:

- 3 cups cooked and mashed sweet potatoes (about 3 medium sweet potatoes)
- 1/4 cup breadcrumbs
- 1/4 cup chopped fresh cilantro
- 1 tablespoon ground flaxseed mixed with 3 tablespoons water (to make a flax egg)
- Salt and pepper to taste
- Vegetable oil for frying

Instructions:

Prepare the BBQ Jackfruit: Use your hands or a fork to shred the jackfruit pieces into smaller strands.

Heat the vegetable oil in a large skillet over medium heat. Add the chopped onion and garlic. Cook until softened, about 2-3 minutes.

Add the shredded jackfruit to the skillet. Cook for 5-7 minutes, stirring occasionally, until the jackfruit starts to brown slightly.

In a bowl, mix together the barbecue sauce, vegetable broth or water, tomato paste, soy sauce or tamari, apple cider vinegar, smoked paprika, ground cumin, salt, and pepper. Pour this sauce over the jackfruit in the skillet.

Reduce the heat to low and simmer the jackfruit in the barbecue sauce mixture for 20-25 minutes, stirring occasionally, until the sauce has thickened and the jackfruit is tender. Remove from heat and set aside.

In a large mixing bowl, combine the cooked and mashed sweet potatoes, breadcrumbs, chopped cilantro, flaxseed mixture (flax egg), salt, and pepper. Mix until well combined.

Fold the BBQ jackfruit mixture into the sweet potato mixture until evenly distributed.

Shape the mixture into patties using your hands. If the mixture is too sticky, you can wet your hands slightly to prevent sticking.

Heat vegetable oil in a large skillet over medium-high heat. Once hot, add the patties to the skillet (you may need to work in batches depending on the size of your skillet). Cook for 3-4 minutes on each side, or until golden brown and crispy.

Once cooked, transfer the BBQ jackfruit patties to a plate lined with paper towels to drain any excess oil.

Serve the BBQ jackfruit patties hot, optionally with additional barbecue sauce for dipping. Enjoy them as a delicious and flavorful plant-based meal!

Jerk Tofu Turnovers

Ingredients:

For the pastry:

- 3 cups all-purpose flour
- 1 teaspoon salt
- 1 cup cold vegan butter or vegetable shortening
- 1/2 cup ice water

For the jerk tofu filling:

- 1 block (14 oz) extra firm tofu, pressed and diced
- 2 tablespoons jerk seasoning
- 1 tablespoon vegetable oil
- 1 onion, finely chopped
- 2 cloves garlic, minced
- 1 bell pepper, finely chopped
- 1 cup diced tomatoes
- 1 tablespoon soy sauce or tamari
- 1 tablespoon maple syrup or brown sugar
- 1 tablespoon apple cider vinegar
- Salt and pepper to taste
- Optional: chopped fresh cilantro for garnish

Instructions:

Preheat the oven to 375°F (190°C). Line a baking sheet with parchment paper.
To make the pastry, sift the flour and salt together in a large mixing bowl. Cut the cold vegan butter or shortening into small cubes and add them to the flour mixture.
Use your fingers or a pastry cutter to rub the butter into the flour until the mixture resembles coarse crumbs.
Gradually add the ice water, a little at a time, mixing until a dough forms. Be careful not to overwork the dough. Shape the dough into a ball, wrap it in plastic wrap, and refrigerate for at least 30 minutes.
While the dough is chilling, prepare the jerk tofu filling. In a bowl, toss the diced tofu with the jerk seasoning until evenly coated.

Heat the vegetable oil in a skillet over medium heat. Add the chopped onion and garlic. Cook until softened, about 2-3 minutes.

Add the seasoned tofu to the skillet. Cook for 5-7 minutes, stirring occasionally, until the tofu is browned on all sides.

Stir in the chopped bell pepper and diced tomatoes. Cook for another 2-3 minutes.

Add the soy sauce or tamari, maple syrup or brown sugar, apple cider vinegar, salt, and pepper. Stir well to combine. Cook for another 2-3 minutes, then remove from heat.

Remove the chilled dough from the refrigerator. Roll it out on a lightly floured surface to about 1/8 inch thickness. Use a round cutter or a small bowl to cut out circles, approximately 5-6 inches in diameter.

Place a spoonful of the jerk tofu filling in the center of each pastry circle. Fold the dough over the filling to form a half-moon shape and crimp the edges with a fork to seal.

Place the assembled turnovers on the prepared baking sheet. Bake in the preheated oven for 25-30 minutes, or until the pastry is golden brown and cooked through.

Garnish the jerk tofu turnovers with chopped fresh cilantro before serving. Enjoy them warm as a flavorful and satisfying snack or meal!

Beef and Cheese Patties

Ingredients:

For the pastry:

- 3 cups all-purpose flour
- 1 teaspoon salt
- 1 cup cold vegan butter or vegetable shortening
- 1/2 cup ice water

For the beef and cheese filling:

- 1 tablespoon vegetable oil
- 1 onion, finely chopped
- 2 cloves garlic, minced
- 1 pound ground beef
- 1 teaspoon Worcestershire sauce (vegan if desired)
- 1 teaspoon paprika
- 1/2 teaspoon dried thyme
- Salt and pepper to taste
- 1 cup grated cheese (cheddar, mozzarella, or your choice)
- Optional: chopped fresh parsley for garnish

Instructions:

Preheat the oven to 375°F (190°C). Line a baking sheet with parchment paper.
To make the pastry, sift the flour and salt together in a large mixing bowl. Cut the cold vegan butter or shortening into small cubes and add them to the flour mixture.
Use your fingers or a pastry cutter to rub the butter into the flour until the mixture resembles coarse crumbs.
Gradually add the ice water, a little at a time, mixing until a dough forms. Be careful not to overwork the dough. Shape the dough into a ball, wrap it in plastic wrap, and refrigerate for at least 30 minutes.
While the dough is chilling, prepare the beef and cheese filling. Heat the vegetable oil in a skillet over medium heat. Add the chopped onion and garlic. Cook until softened, about 2-3 minutes.

Add the ground beef to the skillet. Cook, breaking it apart with a spoon, until browned and cooked through, about 5-7 minutes.

Stir in the Worcestershire sauce, paprika, dried thyme, salt, and pepper. Cook for another 2-3 minutes to allow the flavors to meld together. Remove from heat and let the filling cool slightly.

Remove the chilled dough from the refrigerator. Roll it out on a lightly floured surface to about 1/8 inch thickness. Use a round cutter or a small bowl to cut out circles, approximately 5-6 inches in diameter.

Place a spoonful of the beef and cheese filling in the center of each pastry circle. Sprinkle some grated cheese over the filling.

Fold the dough over the filling to form a half-moon shape and crimp the edges with a fork to seal.

Place the assembled patties on the prepared baking sheet. Bake in the preheated oven for 25-30 minutes, or until the pastry is golden brown and cooked through.

Garnish the beef and cheese patties with chopped fresh parsley before serving. Enjoy them warm as a delicious snack or meal!

Jerk Pork Turnovers

Ingredients:

For the Filling:

- 1 lb (450g) boneless pork shoulder, diced into small pieces
- 2 tablespoons Jamaican jerk seasoning
- 2 tablespoons olive oil
- 1 onion, finely chopped
- 2 cloves garlic, minced
- 1 bell pepper, diced
- 1/2 cup pineapple, diced
- Salt and pepper to taste
- 2 tablespoons chopped fresh cilantro

For the Dough:

- 2 cups all-purpose flour
- 1/2 teaspoon salt
- 1/2 cup cold butter, cut into small cubes
- 1/2 cup cold water

Instructions:

Preheat the oven to 375°F (190°C).
In a bowl, toss the diced pork shoulder with Jamaican jerk seasoning until evenly coated.
Heat olive oil in a skillet over medium heat. Add the seasoned pork and cook until browned on all sides, about 5-7 minutes. Remove the pork from the skillet and set aside.
In the same skillet, add chopped onion and cook until softened, about 3-4 minutes. Add minced garlic and cook for another minute.
Stir in diced bell pepper and cook for 2-3 minutes until slightly softened.
Return the cooked pork to the skillet and add diced pineapple. Cook for another 2-3 minutes until everything is heated through. Season with salt and pepper to taste. Stir in chopped fresh cilantro. Remove from heat and let the filling cool slightly.

In a large mixing bowl, combine all-purpose flour and salt. Add cold butter cubes and rub them into the flour using your fingertips until the mixture resembles coarse crumbs.

Gradually add cold water, a little at a time, and mix until the dough comes together. You may not need to use all the water.

Transfer the dough onto a floured surface and knead it gently until smooth. Roll out the dough to about 1/8 inch (3mm) thickness.

Use a round cutter or a small plate to cut out circles from the dough.

Place a spoonful of the pork filling onto one half of each dough circle, leaving a small border around the edges.

Fold the other half of the dough over the filling to form a half-circle shape. Press the edges together firmly to seal. You can use a fork to crimp the edges for decoration.

Transfer the filled turnovers onto a baking sheet lined with parchment paper.

Bake in the preheated oven for 20-25 minutes, or until the turnovers are golden brown and crispy.

Remove from the oven and let the turnovers cool slightly before serving.

Enjoy your homemade Jerk Pork Turnovers as a delicious snack or appetizer!

Coconut Curry Vegetable Patties

Ingredients:

For the Filling:

- 2 tablespoons coconut oil
- 1 small onion, finely chopped
- 2 cloves garlic, minced
- 1 small carrot, grated
- 1 small zucchini, grated
- 1 small bell pepper, finely chopped
- 1 cup cooked chickpeas, mashed
- 1 tablespoon curry powder
- 1 teaspoon ground cumin
- 1/2 teaspoon ground turmeric
- 1/2 teaspoon ground coriander
- Salt and pepper to taste
- 1/4 cup coconut milk
- 2 tablespoons chopped fresh cilantro

For the Dough:

- 2 cups all-purpose flour
- 1 teaspoon salt
- 1/2 cup coconut oil or vegan butter, chilled and cubed
- 1/2 cup cold water

Instructions:

In a skillet, heat coconut oil over medium heat. Add chopped onion and minced garlic and sauté until softened, about 2-3 minutes.
Add grated carrot, grated zucchini, and chopped bell pepper to the skillet. Cook for another 3-4 minutes, until the vegetables are tender.
Stir in mashed chickpeas, curry powder, ground cumin, ground turmeric, ground coriander, salt, and pepper. Cook for 2-3 minutes, allowing the flavors to meld together.

Pour in coconut milk and simmer for 2-3 minutes until the mixture is thickened. Remove from heat and stir in chopped fresh cilantro. Let the filling cool slightly.
In a large mixing bowl, combine all-purpose flour and salt. Add chilled and cubed coconut oil or vegan butter. Rub the fat into the flour using your fingertips until the mixture resembles coarse crumbs.
Gradually add cold water, a little at a time, and mix until the dough comes together. You may not need to use all the water.
Transfer the dough onto a floured surface and knead it gently until smooth.
Divide the dough into equal portions and shape each portion into a ball.
Roll out each dough ball into a circle about 1/8 inch (3mm) thick.
Place a spoonful of the vegetable filling onto one half of each dough circle, leaving a small border around the edges.
Fold the other half of the dough over the filling to form a half-circle shape. Press the edges together firmly to seal. You can use a fork to crimp the edges for decoration.
Repeat with the remaining dough and filling.
Place the filled patties onto a baking sheet lined with parchment paper.
Preheat your oven to 375°F (190°C). Bake the patties for 20-25 minutes, or until golden brown and crispy.
Remove from the oven and let the patties cool slightly before serving.

Enjoy your homemade Coconut Curry Vegetable Patties as a delicious snack or appetizer!

Lobster and Shrimp Turnovers

Ingredients:

For the Filling:

- 1 tablespoon olive oil
- 1 small onion, finely chopped
- 2 cloves garlic, minced
- 8 oz (225g) cooked lobster meat, chopped
- 8 oz (225g) cooked shrimp, chopped
- 1/2 cup diced bell pepper (any color)
- 1/4 cup diced celery
- 1/4 cup diced carrot
- 1/4 cup frozen peas
- 2 tablespoons all-purpose flour
- 1 cup vegetable broth
- 1/4 cup heavy cream or coconut cream
- 1 tablespoon chopped fresh parsley
- Salt and pepper to taste

For the Dough:

- 2 cups all-purpose flour
- 1/2 teaspoon salt
- 1/2 cup cold butter, cubed
- 1/4 cup cold water

Instructions:

In a skillet, heat olive oil over medium heat. Add chopped onion and minced garlic and sauté until softened, about 2-3 minutes.
Add diced bell pepper, diced celery, and diced carrot to the skillet. Cook for another 3-4 minutes, until the vegetables are tender.
Stir in chopped lobster meat and chopped shrimp. Cook for 2-3 minutes, until heated through.
Sprinkle all-purpose flour over the seafood and vegetable mixture, stirring to combine.

Gradually pour in vegetable broth and heavy cream or coconut cream, stirring constantly. Cook until the mixture thickens, about 3-4 minutes.

Stir in frozen peas and chopped fresh parsley. Season with salt and pepper to taste. Remove from heat and let the filling cool slightly.

In a large mixing bowl, combine all-purpose flour and salt. Add cold butter cubes and rub them into the flour using your fingertips until the mixture resembles coarse crumbs.

Gradually add cold water, a little at a time, and mix until the dough comes together. You may not need to use all the water.

Transfer the dough onto a floured surface and knead it gently until smooth. Roll out the dough to about 1/8 inch (3mm) thickness.

Use a round cutter or a small plate to cut out circles from the dough.

Place a spoonful of the seafood and vegetable filling onto one half of each dough circle, leaving a small border around the edges.

Fold the other half of the dough over the filling to form a half-circle shape. Press the edges together firmly to seal. You can use a fork to crimp the edges for decoration.

Transfer the filled turnovers onto a baking sheet lined with parchment paper. Preheat your oven to 375°F (190°C). Bake the turnovers for 20-25 minutes, or until golden brown and crispy.

Remove from the oven and let the turnovers cool slightly before serving.

Enjoy your homemade Lobster and Shrimp Turnovers as a delicious appetizer or snack!

Plantain and Black Bean Patties

Ingredients:

For the Patties:

- 2 ripe plantains, peeled and mashed
- 1 can (15 oz) black beans, drained and rinsed
- 1 small onion, finely chopped
- 2 cloves garlic, minced
- 1/4 cup breadcrumbs (gluten-free if needed)
- 2 tablespoons chopped fresh cilantro
- 1 teaspoon ground cumin
- 1/2 teaspoon smoked paprika
- Salt and pepper to taste
- 2 tablespoons olive oil, for frying

For the Avocado Crema:

- 1 ripe avocado, peeled and pitted
- 1/4 cup plain vegan yogurt
- 1 tablespoon lime juice
- Salt and pepper to taste

Instructions:

In a large mixing bowl, combine mashed plantains, black beans, chopped onion, minced garlic, breadcrumbs, chopped fresh cilantro, ground cumin, smoked paprika, salt, and pepper. Mix until well combined.
Form the mixture into patties using your hands, shaping them into uniform rounds.
Heat olive oil in a skillet over medium heat. Add the patties to the skillet and cook for about 4-5 minutes on each side, or until golden brown and heated through. You may need to cook them in batches depending on the size of your skillet.
While the patties are cooking, prepare the avocado crema. In a blender or food processor, combine ripe avocado, vegan yogurt, lime juice, salt, and pepper. Blend until smooth and creamy.

Once the patties are cooked, remove them from the skillet and place them on a plate lined with paper towels to absorb any excess oil.

Serve the Plantain and Black Bean Patties hot, topped with a dollop of avocado crema.

Enjoy as a delicious appetizer, snack, or part of a main meal!

These Plantain and Black Bean Patties are flavorful, satisfying, and perfect for a variety of occasions. The creamy avocado crema adds a refreshing touch to complement the savory patties. Enjoy!

Callaloo and Corn Turnovers

Ingredients:

For the Filling:

- 2 cups callaloo leaves, chopped (substitute with spinach if callaloo is not available)
- 1 cup corn kernels (fresh, frozen, or canned)
- 1 small onion, finely chopped
- 2 cloves garlic, minced
- 1/2 teaspoon dried thyme
- 1/4 teaspoon ground allspice
- Salt and pepper to taste
- 1 tablespoon olive oil

For the Dough:

- 2 cups all-purpose flour
- 1/2 teaspoon salt
- 1/2 cup cold butter, cubed
- 1/2 cup cold water

Instructions:

In a skillet, heat olive oil over medium heat. Add chopped onion and minced garlic and sauté until softened, about 2-3 minutes.

Add chopped callaloo leaves (or spinach) to the skillet and cook until wilted, about 3-4 minutes.

Stir in corn kernels, dried thyme, ground allspice, salt, and pepper. Cook for another 2-3 minutes until everything is heated through. Remove from heat and let the filling cool slightly.

In a large mixing bowl, combine all-purpose flour and salt. Add chilled and cubed butter. Rub the butter into the flour using your fingertips until the mixture resembles coarse crumbs.

Gradually add cold water, a little at a time, and mix until the dough comes together. You may not need to use all the water.

Transfer the dough onto a floured surface and knead it gently until smooth.
Divide the dough into equal portions and shape each portion into a ball.
Roll out each dough ball into a circle about 1/8 inch (3mm) thick.
Place a spoonful of the callaloo and corn filling onto one half of each dough circle, leaving a small border around the edges.
Fold the other half of the dough over the filling to form a half-circle shape. Press the edges together firmly to seal. You can use a fork to crimp the edges for decoration.
Repeat with the remaining dough and filling.
Place the filled turnovers onto a baking sheet lined with parchment paper.
Preheat your oven to 375°F (190°C). Bake the turnovers for 20-25 minutes, or until golden brown and crispy.
Remove from the oven and let the turnovers cool slightly before serving.

Enjoy your homemade Callaloo and Corn Turnovers as a delicious snack or appetizer!

Spicy Chicken Patties

Ingredients:

For the Patties:

- 1 lb (450g) ground chicken
- 1/2 cup breadcrumbs
- 1/4 cup finely chopped onion
- 2 cloves garlic, minced
- 1 tablespoon chopped fresh cilantro
- 1 teaspoon ground cumin
- 1/2 teaspoon paprika
- 1/2 teaspoon chili powder
- 1/4 teaspoon cayenne pepper (adjust to taste)
- Salt and pepper to taste
- 1 tablespoon olive oil, for frying

For the Spicy Mayo:

- 1/4 cup mayonnaise
- 1 tablespoon sriracha sauce (adjust to taste)
- 1 teaspoon lime juice
- Salt to taste

Instructions:

In a large mixing bowl, combine ground chicken, breadcrumbs, finely chopped onion, minced garlic, chopped fresh cilantro, ground cumin, paprika, chili powder, cayenne pepper, salt, and pepper. Mix until well combined.
Form the mixture into patties using your hands, shaping them into uniform rounds.
Heat olive oil in a skillet over medium heat. Add the patties to the skillet and cook for about 4-5 minutes on each side, or until golden brown and cooked through. Make sure the internal temperature reaches 165°F (74°C).
While the patties are cooking, prepare the spicy mayo. In a small bowl, combine mayonnaise, sriracha sauce, lime juice, and salt. Stir until well combined.

Once the patties are cooked, remove them from the skillet and place them on a plate lined with paper towels to absorb any excess oil.

Serve the Spicy Chicken Patties hot, topped with a dollop of spicy mayo.

Enjoy as a delicious appetizer, snack, or part of a main meal!

These Spicy Chicken Patties are flavorful, juicy, and perfect for adding a kick to your meal. The creamy and tangy spicy mayo complements the heat of the patties perfectly. Enjoy!

Saltfish and Okra Turnovers

Ingredients:

For the Filling:

- 1 cup salted codfish (saltfish), soaked overnight and shredded
- 1 cup chopped okra
- 1 small onion, finely chopped
- 2 cloves garlic, minced
- 1 medium tomato, chopped
- 1/4 cup chopped bell pepper (any color)
- 1/4 cup chopped fresh cilantro
- 1/4 teaspoon ground black pepper
- 1/4 teaspoon dried thyme
- 1 tablespoon olive oil

For the Dough:

- 2 cups all-purpose flour
- 1/2 teaspoon salt
- 1/2 cup cold butter, cubed
- 1/4 cup cold water

Instructions:

In a skillet, heat olive oil over medium heat. Add chopped onion and minced garlic and sauté until softened, about 2-3 minutes.
Add shredded saltfish to the skillet and cook for about 5 minutes, stirring occasionally.
Stir in chopped okra, chopped tomato, chopped bell pepper, chopped fresh cilantro, ground black pepper, and dried thyme. Cook for another 5-7 minutes, or until the vegetables are tender.
Remove from heat and let the filling cool slightly.
In a large mixing bowl, combine all-purpose flour and salt. Add chilled and cubed butter. Rub the butter into the flour using your fingertips until the mixture resembles coarse crumbs.

Gradually add cold water, a little at a time, and mix until the dough comes together. You may not need to use all the water.

Transfer the dough onto a floured surface and knead it gently until smooth. Roll out the dough to about 1/8 inch (3mm) thickness.

Use a round cutter or a small plate to cut out circles from the dough.

Place a spoonful of the saltfish and okra filling onto one half of each dough circle, leaving a small border around the edges.

Fold the other half of the dough over the filling to form a half-circle shape. Press the edges together firmly to seal. You can use a fork to crimp the edges for decoration.

Repeat with the remaining dough and filling.

Place the filled turnovers onto a baking sheet lined with parchment paper.

Preheat your oven to 375°F (190°C). Bake the turnovers for 20-25 minutes, or until golden brown and crispy.

Remove from the oven and let the turnovers cool slightly before serving.

Enjoy your homemade Saltfish and Okra Turnovers as a delicious snack or appetizer!

Vegan Chickpea Patties

Ingredients:

- 2 cans (15 oz each) chickpeas, drained and rinsed
- 1 small onion, finely chopped
- 2 cloves garlic, minced
- 1/4 cup chopped fresh parsley
- 2 tablespoons chopped fresh cilantro
- 2 tablespoons lemon juice
- 1 teaspoon ground cumin
- 1/2 teaspoon ground coriander
- 1/4 teaspoon smoked paprika
- Salt and pepper to taste
- 2 tablespoons all-purpose flour (or chickpea flour for gluten-free option)
- 2 tablespoons olive oil, for frying

Instructions:

In a food processor, combine the drained and rinsed chickpeas, chopped onion, minced garlic, chopped fresh parsley, chopped fresh cilantro, lemon juice, ground cumin, ground coriander, smoked paprika, salt, and pepper. Pulse until the mixture is well combined but still slightly chunky. You may need to scrape down the sides of the food processor a few times.

Transfer the chickpea mixture to a mixing bowl. Stir in the all-purpose flour until well combined. If the mixture seems too wet, you can add a little more flour to help bind it together.

Heat olive oil in a skillet over medium heat.

While the oil is heating, shape the chickpea mixture into patties using your hands, shaping them into uniform rounds.

Once the oil is hot, add the chickpea patties to the skillet, working in batches if necessary to avoid overcrowding the pan. Cook for about 4-5 minutes on each side, or until golden brown and crispy.

Once the patties are cooked, remove them from the skillet and place them on a plate lined with paper towels to absorb any excess oil.

Serve the Vegan Chickpea Patties hot, with your favorite dipping sauce or toppings.

Enjoy these flavorful and protein-packed patties as a delicious and satisfying meal or snack!

These Vegan Chickpea Patties are versatile and can be enjoyed in sandwiches, salads, wraps, or simply on their own. They are perfect for meal prep and can be stored in the refrigerator for several days. Enjoy!

Mango Curry Chicken Turnovers

Ingredients:

For the Filling:

- 1 lb (450g) cooked chicken breast, diced
- 1 ripe mango, peeled, pitted, and diced
- 1 small onion, finely chopped
- 2 cloves garlic, minced
- 1 tablespoon curry powder
- 1/2 teaspoon ground cumin
- 1/2 teaspoon ground coriander
- 1/4 teaspoon turmeric
- 1/4 teaspoon cayenne pepper (adjust to taste)
- Salt and pepper to taste
- 2 tablespoons olive oil

For the Dough:

- 2 cups all-purpose flour
- 1/2 teaspoon salt
- 1/2 cup cold butter, cubed
- 1/2 cup cold water

Instructions:

In a skillet, heat olive oil over medium heat. Add chopped onion and minced garlic and sauté until softened, about 2-3 minutes.
Add diced chicken breast to the skillet and cook until heated through.
Stir in diced mango, curry powder, ground cumin, ground coriander, turmeric, cayenne pepper, salt, and pepper. Cook for another 2-3 minutes, until the flavors meld together. Remove from heat and let the filling cool slightly.
In a large mixing bowl, combine all-purpose flour and salt. Add chilled and cubed butter. Rub the butter into the flour using your fingertips until the mixture resembles coarse crumbs.
Gradually add cold water, a little at a time, and mix until the dough comes together. You may not need to use all the water.

Transfer the dough onto a floured surface and knead it gently until smooth. Roll out the dough to about 1/8 inch (3mm) thickness.

Use a round cutter or a small plate to cut out circles from the dough.

Place a spoonful of the mango curry chicken filling onto one half of each dough circle, leaving a small border around the edges.

Fold the other half of the dough over the filling to form a half-circle shape. Press the edges together firmly to seal. You can use a fork to crimp the edges for decoration.

Repeat with the remaining dough and filling.

Place the filled turnovers onto a baking sheet lined with parchment paper.

Preheat your oven to 375°F (190°C). Bake the turnovers for 20-25 minutes, or until golden brown and crispy.

Remove from the oven and let the turnovers cool slightly before serving.

Enjoy your homemade Mango Curry Chicken Turnovers as a delicious snack or appetizer!

Jamaican Pumpkin Patties

Ingredients:

For the Filling:

- 2 cups mashed pumpkin (cooked and drained)
- 1 small onion, finely chopped
- 2 cloves garlic, minced
- 1/2 cup cooked chickpeas, mashed
- 1/4 cup chopped bell pepper (any color)
- 1/4 cup chopped fresh cilantro
- 1 tablespoon curry powder
- 1/2 teaspoon ground cumin
- 1/4 teaspoon ground cinnamon
- 1/4 teaspoon ground nutmeg
- 1/4 teaspoon cayenne pepper (adjust to taste)
- Salt and pepper to taste
- 2 tablespoons olive oil

For the Dough:

- 2 cups all-purpose flour
- 1/2 teaspoon salt
- 1/2 cup cold butter or vegetable shortening, cubed
- 1/2 cup cold water

Instructions:

In a skillet, heat olive oil over medium heat. Add chopped onion and minced garlic and sauté until softened, about 2-3 minutes.

Add mashed pumpkin, mashed chickpeas, chopped bell pepper, chopped fresh cilantro, curry powder, ground cumin, ground cinnamon, ground nutmeg, cayenne pepper, salt, and pepper to the skillet. Cook for another 5-7 minutes, stirring occasionally, until the mixture is heated through and well combined. Remove from heat and let the filling cool slightly.

In a large mixing bowl, combine all-purpose flour and salt. Add chilled and cubed butter or vegetable shortening. Rub the fat into the flour using your fingertips until the mixture resembles coarse crumbs.

Gradually add cold water, a little at a time, and mix until the dough comes together. You may not need to use all the water.

Transfer the dough onto a floured surface and knead it gently until smooth. Roll out the dough to about 1/8 inch (3mm) thickness.

Use a round cutter or a small plate to cut out circles from the dough.

Place a spoonful of the pumpkin filling onto one half of each dough circle, leaving a small border around the edges.

Fold the other half of the dough over the filling to form a half-circle shape. Press the edges together firmly to seal. You can use a fork to crimp the edges for decoration.

Repeat with the remaining dough and filling.

Place the filled turnovers onto a baking sheet lined with parchment paper.

Preheat your oven to 375°F (190°C). Bake the turnovers for 20-25 minutes, or until golden brown and crispy.

Remove from the oven and let the turnovers cool slightly before serving.

Enjoy your homemade Jamaican Pumpkin Patties as a delicious snack or appetizer!

Escovitch Fish Turnovers

Ingredients:

For the Filling:

- 1 lb (450g) white fish fillets (such as snapper, tilapia, or cod), cut into small cubes
- 1 small onion, thinly sliced
- 1 bell pepper (any color), thinly sliced
- 2 cloves garlic, minced
- 1/4 cup chopped scallions
- 1/4 cup chopped fresh parsley
- 1/4 cup white vinegar
- 2 tablespoons vegetable oil
- 1 teaspoon ground allspice
- 1 teaspoon dried thyme
- Salt and pepper to taste
- 1 tablespoon flour (for thickening, optional)

For the Dough:

- 2 cups all-purpose flour
- 1/2 teaspoon salt
- 1/2 cup cold butter, cubed
- 1/2 cup cold water

Instructions:

In a skillet, heat vegetable oil over medium heat. Add thinly sliced onion, thinly sliced bell pepper, and minced garlic. Sauté until softened, about 3-4 minutes. Add cubed fish fillets to the skillet and cook until they are just cooked through, about 4-5 minutes. Be careful not to overcook the fish. Remove from heat.
Stir in chopped scallions, chopped fresh parsley, white vinegar, ground allspice, dried thyme, salt, and pepper. If the mixture is too liquidy, you can sprinkle flour over the filling to thicken it. Stir until well combined. Let the filling cool slightly.
In a large mixing bowl, combine all-purpose flour and salt. Add chilled and cubed butter. Rub the butter into the flour using your fingertips until the mixture resembles coarse crumbs.

Gradually add cold water, a little at a time, and mix until the dough comes together. You may not need to use all the water.

Transfer the dough onto a floured surface and knead it gently until smooth. Roll out the dough to about 1/8 inch (3mm) thickness.

Use a round cutter or a small plate to cut out circles from the dough.

Place a spoonful of the escovitch fish filling onto one half of each dough circle, leaving a small border around the edges.

Fold the other half of the dough over the filling to form a half-circle shape. Press the edges together firmly to seal. You can use a fork to crimp the edges for decoration.

Repeat with the remaining dough and filling.

Place the filled turnovers onto a baking sheet lined with parchment paper.

Preheat your oven to 375°F (190°C). Bake the turnovers for 20-25 minutes, or until golden brown and crispy.

Remove from the oven and let the turnovers cool slightly before serving.

Enjoy your homemade Escovitch Fish Turnovers as a delicious snack or appetizer!

Curry Chickpea Patties

Ingredients:

For the Patties:

- 2 cans (15 oz each) chickpeas, drained and rinsed
- 1 small onion, finely chopped
- 2 cloves garlic, minced
- 1 tablespoon curry powder
- 1 teaspoon ground cumin
- 1/2 teaspoon ground coriander
- 1/4 teaspoon turmeric
- 1/4 teaspoon cayenne pepper (adjust to taste)
- Salt and pepper to taste
- 2 tablespoons chopped fresh cilantro
- 2 tablespoons all-purpose flour (or chickpea flour for gluten-free option)
- 2 tablespoons olive oil, for frying

Instructions:

In a food processor, combine the drained and rinsed chickpeas, chopped onion, minced garlic, curry powder, ground cumin, ground coriander, turmeric, cayenne pepper, salt, and pepper. Pulse until the mixture is coarsely ground but still has some texture.

Transfer the chickpea mixture to a mixing bowl. Stir in chopped fresh cilantro and all-purpose flour until well combined. If the mixture seems too wet, you can add a little more flour to help bind it together.

Heat olive oil in a skillet over medium heat.

While the oil is heating, shape the chickpea mixture into patties using your hands, shaping them into uniform rounds.

Once the oil is hot, add the chickpea patties to the skillet, working in batches if necessary to avoid overcrowding the pan. Cook for about 4-5 minutes on each side, or until golden brown and crispy.

Once the patties are cooked, remove them from the skillet and place them on a plate lined with paper towels to absorb any excess oil.

Serve the Curry Chickpea Patties hot, with your favorite dipping sauce or toppings.

Enjoy these flavorful and protein-packed patties as a delicious and satisfying meal or snack!

These Curry Chickpea Patties are versatile and can be enjoyed in sandwiches, salads, wraps, or simply on their own. They are perfect for meal prep and can be stored in the refrigerator for several days. Enjoy!

Spicy Beef Patties

Ingredients:

For the Filling:

- 1 lb (450g) ground beef
- 1 small onion, finely chopped
- 2 cloves garlic, minced
- 1 small bell pepper (any color), finely chopped
- 1 tablespoon curry powder
- 1 teaspoon ground cumin
- 1 teaspoon paprika
- 1/2 teaspoon cayenne pepper (adjust to taste)
- Salt and pepper to taste
- 2 tablespoons chopped fresh cilantro
- 2 tablespoons olive oil

For the Dough:

- 2 cups all-purpose flour
- 1/2 teaspoon salt
- 1/2 cup cold butter, cubed
- 1/2 cup cold water

Instructions:

In a skillet, heat olive oil over medium heat. Add chopped onion and minced garlic and sauté until softened, about 2-3 minutes.
Add ground beef to the skillet and cook until browned, breaking it up with a spoon as it cooks.
Stir in chopped bell pepper, curry powder, ground cumin, paprika, cayenne pepper, salt, and pepper. Cook for another 5-7 minutes, or until the beef is fully cooked and the flavors meld together. Remove from heat and let the filling cool slightly.
In a large mixing bowl, combine all-purpose flour and salt. Add chilled and cubed butter. Rub the butter into the flour using your fingertips until the mixture resembles coarse crumbs.
Gradually add cold water, a little at a time, and mix until the dough comes together. You may not need to use all the water.

Transfer the dough onto a floured surface and knead it gently until smooth. Roll out the dough to about 1/8 inch (3mm) thickness.

Use a round cutter or a small plate to cut out circles from the dough.

Place a spoonful of the spicy beef filling onto one half of each dough circle, leaving a small border around the edges.

Fold the other half of the dough over the filling to form a half-circle shape. Press the edges together firmly to seal. You can use a fork to crimp the edges for decoration.

Repeat with the remaining dough and filling.

Place the filled turnovers onto a baking sheet lined with parchment paper.

Preheat your oven to 375°F (190°C). Bake the turnovers for 20-25 minutes, or until golden brown and crispy.

Remove from the oven and let the turnovers cool slightly before serving.

Enjoy your homemade Spicy Beef Patties as a delicious snack or appetizer!

Jerk Seitan Turnovers

Ingredients:

For the Filling:

- 1 package (8 oz) seitan, diced into small cubes
- 1 small onion, finely chopped
- 2 cloves garlic, minced
- 1 small bell pepper (any color), finely chopped
- 2 tablespoons jerk seasoning
- 1 tablespoon soy sauce or tamari
- 1 tablespoon olive oil

For the Dough:

- 2 cups all-purpose flour
- 1/2 teaspoon salt
- 1/2 cup cold vegan butter, cubed
- 1/4 cup cold water

Instructions:

In a skillet, heat olive oil over medium heat. Add chopped onion and minced garlic and sauté until softened, about 2-3 minutes.
Add diced seitan to the skillet and cook until lightly browned, about 5 minutes.
Stir in chopped bell pepper, jerk seasoning, and soy sauce. Cook for another 3-4 minutes, or until the flavors meld together. Remove from heat and let the filling cool slightly.
In a large mixing bowl, combine all-purpose flour and salt. Add chilled and cubed vegan butter. Rub the butter into the flour using your fingertips until the mixture resembles coarse crumbs.
Gradually add cold water, a little at a time, and mix until the dough comes together. You may not need to use all the water.
Transfer the dough onto a floured surface and knead it gently until smooth. Roll out the dough to about 1/8 inch (3mm) thickness.
Use a round cutter or a small plate to cut out circles from the dough.
Place a spoonful of the jerk seitan filling onto one half of each dough circle, leaving a small border around the edges.

Fold the other half of the dough over the filling to form a half-circle shape. Press the edges together firmly to seal. You can use a fork to crimp the edges for decoration.

Repeat with the remaining dough and filling.

Place the filled turnovers onto a baking sheet lined with parchment paper.

Preheat your oven to 375°F (190°C). Bake the turnovers for 20-25 minutes, or until golden brown and crispy.

Remove from the oven and let the turnovers cool slightly before serving.

Enjoy your homemade Jerk Seitan Turnovers as a delicious snack or appetizer!

Sweet Potato and Chickpea Patties

Ingredients:

- 1 large sweet potato, peeled and diced
- 1 can (15 oz) chickpeas, drained and rinsed
- 1 small onion, finely chopped
- 2 cloves garlic, minced
- 1 teaspoon ground cumin
- 1 teaspoon ground coriander
- 1/2 teaspoon smoked paprika
- 1/4 teaspoon cayenne pepper (adjust to taste)
- Salt and pepper to taste
- 2 tablespoons chopped fresh cilantro
- 2 tablespoons all-purpose flour (or chickpea flour for gluten-free option)
- 2 tablespoons olive oil, for frying

Instructions:

Place diced sweet potato in a pot of boiling water and cook until tender, about 10-15 minutes. Drain and let cool slightly.

In a large mixing bowl, mash the cooked sweet potato with a fork or potato masher. Add the drained and rinsed chickpeas to the bowl and mash them slightly, leaving some texture.

Add finely chopped onion, minced garlic, ground cumin, ground coriander, smoked paprika, cayenne pepper, salt, pepper, and chopped fresh cilantro to the bowl. Mix until well combined.

Stir in all-purpose flour (or chickpea flour) until the mixture holds together well. If the mixture is too wet, you can add a little more flour.

Shape the mixture into patties using your hands, forming them into uniform rounds.

Heat olive oil in a skillet over medium heat. Add the patties to the skillet and cook for about 4-5 minutes on each side, or until golden brown and crispy.

Once the patties are cooked, remove them from the skillet and place them on a plate lined with paper towels to absorb any excess oil.

Serve the Sweet Potato and Chickpea Patties hot, with your favorite dipping sauce or toppings.

Enjoy these flavorful and nutritious patties as a delicious and satisfying meal or snack!

These Sweet Potato and Chickpea Patties are versatile and can be served on their own, in sandwiches, wraps, or salads. They are perfect for meal prep and can be stored in the refrigerator for several days. Enjoy!

Tofu and Vegetable Turnovers

Ingredients:

For the Filling:

- 1 block (14 oz) extra-firm tofu, pressed and diced
- 1 cup mixed vegetables (such as bell peppers, carrots, peas, and corn), diced
- 1 small onion, finely chopped
- 2 cloves garlic, minced
- 2 tablespoons soy sauce or tamari
- 1 tablespoon olive oil
- 1 teaspoon ground ginger
- 1/2 teaspoon ground turmeric
- Salt and pepper to taste
- 2 tablespoons chopped fresh cilantro or green onions (optional)

For the Dough:

- 2 cups all-purpose flour
- 1/2 teaspoon salt
- 1/2 cup cold vegan butter or vegetable shortening, cubed
- 1/4 cup cold water

Instructions:

In a skillet, heat olive oil over medium heat. Add chopped onion and minced garlic and sauté until softened, about 2-3 minutes.
Add diced tofu to the skillet and cook until lightly browned, about 5 minutes.
Stir in diced mixed vegetables, soy sauce or tamari, ground ginger, ground turmeric, salt, and pepper. Cook for another 5-7 minutes, or until the vegetables are tender. Remove from heat and let the filling cool slightly. Stir in chopped fresh cilantro or green onions, if using.
In a large mixing bowl, combine all-purpose flour and salt. Add chilled and cubed vegan butter or vegetable shortening. Rub the fat into the flour using your fingertips until the mixture resembles coarse crumbs.

Gradually add cold water, a little at a time, and mix until the dough comes together. You may not need to use all the water.

Transfer the dough onto a floured surface and knead it gently until smooth. Roll out the dough to about 1/8 inch (3mm) thickness.

Use a round cutter or a small plate to cut out circles from the dough.

Place a spoonful of the tofu and vegetable filling onto one half of each dough circle, leaving a small border around the edges.

Fold the other half of the dough over the filling to form a half-circle shape. Press the edges together firmly to seal. You can use a fork to crimp the edges for decoration.

Repeat with the remaining dough and filling.

Place the filled turnovers onto a baking sheet lined with parchment paper.

Preheat your oven to 375°F (190°C). Bake the turnovers for 20-25 minutes, or until golden brown and crispy.

Remove from the oven and let the turnovers cool slightly before serving.

Enjoy your homemade Tofu and Vegetable Turnovers as a delicious snack or appetizer!

Curried Lamb Patties

Ingredients:

For the Patties:

- 1 lb (450g) ground lamb
- 1 small onion, finely chopped
- 2 cloves garlic, minced
- 1 tablespoon curry powder
- 1 teaspoon ground cumin
- 1 teaspoon ground coriander
- 1/2 teaspoon ground turmeric
- 1/4 teaspoon cayenne pepper (adjust to taste)
- Salt and pepper to taste
- 2 tablespoons chopped fresh cilantro
- 2 tablespoons breadcrumbs (optional, for binding)
- 2 tablespoons olive oil, for frying

Instructions:

In a large mixing bowl, combine the ground lamb, finely chopped onion, minced garlic, curry powder, ground cumin, ground coriander, ground turmeric, cayenne pepper, salt, pepper, and chopped fresh cilantro. Mix well until all the ingredients are evenly distributed.
If the mixture seems too wet, you can add breadcrumbs to help bind it together.
Divide the mixture into equal portions and shape each portion into a patty.
Heat olive oil in a skillet over medium heat.
Once the oil is hot, add the lamb patties to the skillet, working in batches if necessary to avoid overcrowding the pan. Cook for about 4-5 minutes on each side, or until browned and cooked through. Make sure the internal temperature reaches at least 160°F (71°C).
Once the patties are cooked, remove them from the skillet and place them on a plate lined with paper towels to absorb any excess oil.
Serve the Curried Lamb Patties hot, garnished with additional fresh cilantro if desired.
Enjoy these flavorful and aromatic patties as a delicious main dish or appetizer!

These Curried Lamb Patties are packed with spices and flavor, making them a delightful addition to any meal. Serve them with rice, couscous, or a fresh salad for a complete and satisfying dish. Enjoy!

Callaloo and Crab Turnovers

Ingredients:

For the Filling:

- 1 cup cooked crab meat, shredded
- 1 cup callaloo, chopped (substitute with spinach if callaloo is not available)
- 1 small onion, finely chopped
- 2 cloves garlic, minced
- 1 small tomato, diced
- 1 tablespoon olive oil
- 1/2 teaspoon dried thyme
- Salt and pepper to taste
- Hot pepper sauce (optional, to taste)

For the Dough:

- 2 cups all-purpose flour
- 1/2 teaspoon salt
- 1/2 cup cold butter, cubed
- 1/4 cup cold water

Instructions:

In a skillet, heat olive oil over medium heat. Add chopped onion and minced garlic and sauté until softened, about 2-3 minutes.
Add diced tomato to the skillet and cook until softened, about 3-4 minutes.
Stir in cooked crab meat and chopped callaloo (or spinach) to the skillet. Cook for another 5-7 minutes, or until the callaloo is wilted and the mixture is well combined. Season with dried thyme, salt, pepper, and hot pepper sauce (if using). Remove from heat and let the filling cool slightly.
In a large mixing bowl, combine all-purpose flour and salt. Add chilled and cubed butter. Rub the butter into the flour using your fingertips until the mixture resembles coarse crumbs.
Gradually add cold water, a little at a time, and mix until the dough comes together. You may not need to use all the water.
Transfer the dough onto a floured surface and knead it gently until smooth. Roll out the dough to about 1/8 inch (3mm) thickness.

Use a round cutter or a small plate to cut out circles from the dough.

Place a spoonful of the callaloo and crab filling onto one half of each dough circle, leaving a small border around the edges.

Fold the other half of the dough over the filling to form a half-circle shape. Press the edges together firmly to seal. You can use a fork to crimp the edges for decoration.

Repeat with the remaining dough and filling.

Place the filled turnovers onto a baking sheet lined with parchment paper.

Preheat your oven to 375°F (190°C). Bake the turnovers for 20-25 minutes, or until golden brown and crispy.

Remove from the oven and let the turnovers cool slightly before serving.

Enjoy your homemade Callaloo and Crab Turnovers as a delicious snack or appetizer!

Pineapple Teriyaki Chicken Patties

Ingredients:

For the Patties:

- 1 lb (450g) ground chicken
- 1 cup fresh pineapple, finely chopped
- 1 small onion, finely chopped
- 2 cloves garlic, minced
- 2 tablespoons teriyaki sauce
- 1 tablespoon soy sauce or tamari
- 1 teaspoon sesame oil
- 1/4 cup breadcrumbs
- Salt and pepper to taste
- 2 tablespoons chopped fresh cilantro or green onions (optional)
- 2 tablespoons olive oil, for frying

Instructions:

In a large mixing bowl, combine the ground chicken, finely chopped pineapple, finely chopped onion, minced garlic, teriyaki sauce, soy sauce or tamari, sesame oil, breadcrumbs, salt, pepper, and chopped fresh cilantro or green onions (if using). Mix well until all the ingredients are evenly distributed.
Divide the mixture into equal portions and shape each portion into a patty.
Heat olive oil in a skillet over medium heat.
Once the oil is hot, add the chicken patties to the skillet, working in batches if necessary to avoid overcrowding the pan. Cook for about 4-5 minutes on each side, or until golden brown and cooked through. Make sure the internal temperature reaches at least 165°F (74°C).
Once the patties are cooked, remove them from the skillet and place them on a plate lined with paper towels to absorb any excess oil.
Serve the Pineapple Teriyaki Chicken Patties hot, garnished with additional fresh cilantro or green onions if desired.
Enjoy these delicious and juicy patties as a tasty main dish or sandwich filling!

These Pineapple Teriyaki Chicken Patties are bursting with flavor from the sweet pineapple and savory teriyaki sauce. Serve them with rice, noodles, or on a bun with your favorite toppings for a delightful meal!

Saltfish and Potato Turnovers

Ingredients:

For the Filling:

- 1 cup salted codfish (saltfish), soaked and shredded
- 2 large potatoes, peeled and diced
- 1 small onion, finely chopped
- 2 cloves garlic, minced
- 1 small tomato, diced
- 1/2 teaspoon dried thyme
- 1/4 teaspoon black pepper
- 1/4 teaspoon paprika
- 1 tablespoon olive oil

For the Dough:

- 2 cups all-purpose flour
- 1/2 teaspoon salt
- 1/2 cup cold butter, cubed
- 1/4 cup cold water

Instructions:

Start by soaking the salted codfish (saltfish) in cold water for about 8 hours or overnight. Change the water several times during soaking to remove excess salt. After soaking, drain the codfish and shred it into small pieces.

In a pot of boiling water, cook the diced potatoes until they are fork-tender, about 10-15 minutes. Drain and set aside.

In a skillet, heat olive oil over medium heat. Add chopped onion and minced garlic and sauté until softened, about 2-3 minutes.

Add shredded saltfish and diced tomato to the skillet. Cook for another 5 minutes, stirring occasionally.

Stir in cooked diced potatoes, dried thyme, black pepper, and paprika. Cook for another 3-4 minutes, stirring occasionally, until the flavors meld together. Remove from heat and let the filling cool slightly.

In a large mixing bowl, combine all-purpose flour and salt. Add chilled and cubed butter. Rub the butter into the flour using your fingertips until the mixture resembles coarse crumbs.

Gradually add cold water, a little at a time, and mix until the dough comes together. You may not need to use all the water.

Transfer the dough onto a floured surface and knead it gently until smooth. Roll out the dough to about 1/8 inch (3mm) thickness.

Use a round cutter or a small plate to cut out circles from the dough.

Place a spoonful of the saltfish and potato filling onto one half of each dough circle, leaving a small border around the edges.

Fold the other half of the dough over the filling to form a half-circle shape. Press the edges together firmly to seal. You can use a fork to crimp the edges for decoration.

Repeat with the remaining dough and filling.

Place the filled turnovers onto a baking sheet lined with parchment paper.

Preheat your oven to 375°F (190°C). Bake the turnovers for 20-25 minutes, or until golden brown and crispy.

Remove from the oven and let the turnovers cool slightly before serving.

Enjoy your homemade Saltfish and Potato Turnovers as a delicious snack or appetizer!

Vegan BBQ Jackfruit Patties

Ingredients:

For the Patties:

- 2 cans (20 oz each) young green jackfruit in brine or water, drained and shredded
- 1 small onion, finely chopped
- 2 cloves garlic, minced
- 1/2 cup breadcrumbs (gluten-free if needed)
- 2 tablespoons ground flaxseed meal
- 6 tablespoons water
- 2 tablespoons barbecue sauce
- 1 teaspoon smoked paprika
- 1 teaspoon garlic powder
- 1 teaspoon onion powder
- Salt and pepper to taste
- 2 tablespoons olive oil, for frying

For Serving (optional):

- Burger buns
- Lettuce
- Tomato slices
- Red onion slices
- Additional barbecue sauce

Instructions:

In a small bowl, mix together the ground flaxseed meal and water. Let it sit for a few minutes to thicken and form a flax egg.

In a large mixing bowl, combine the shredded jackfruit, finely chopped onion, minced garlic, breadcrumbs, barbecue sauce, smoked paprika, garlic powder, onion powder, salt, pepper, and the prepared flax egg. Mix well until all the ingredients are evenly distributed.

Use your hands to shape the mixture into patties. If the mixture is too wet to hold its shape, you can add more breadcrumbs as needed.

Heat olive oil in a skillet over medium heat.

Once the oil is hot, add the jackfruit patties to the skillet, working in batches if necessary to avoid overcrowding the pan. Cook for about 4-5 minutes on each side, or until golden brown and crispy.

Once the patties are cooked, remove them from the skillet and place them on a plate lined with paper towels to absorb any excess oil.

Serve the Vegan BBQ Jackfruit Patties on burger buns with lettuce, tomato slices, red onion slices, and additional barbecue sauce if desired.

Enjoy these flavorful and satisfying patties as a delicious vegan alternative to traditional barbecue burgers!

These Vegan BBQ Jackfruit Patties are perfect for summer cookouts or any time you're craving a hearty and delicious plant-based meal. Enjoy!

Ackee and Ackee Turnovers

Ingredients:

For the Filling:

- 2 cups canned ackee, drained
- 1 small onion, finely chopped
- 2 cloves garlic, minced
- 1 small tomato, diced
- 1/2 teaspoon dried thyme
- 1/4 teaspoon black pepper
- 1/4 teaspoon paprika
- Salt to taste
- 2 tablespoons olive oil

For the Dough:

- 2 cups all-purpose flour
- 1/2 teaspoon salt
- 1/2 cup cold butter, cubed
- 1/4 cup cold water

Instructions:

In a skillet, heat olive oil over medium heat. Add chopped onion and minced garlic and sauté until softened, about 2-3 minutes.

Add diced tomato to the skillet and cook until softened, about 3-4 minutes.

Stir in canned ackee, dried thyme, black pepper, paprika, and salt. Cook for another 5 minutes, stirring occasionally, until the flavors meld together. Remove from heat and let the filling cool slightly.

In a large mixing bowl, combine all-purpose flour and salt. Add chilled and cubed butter. Rub the butter into the flour using your fingertips until the mixture resembles coarse crumbs.

Gradually add cold water, a little at a time, and mix until the dough comes together. You may not need to use all the water.

Transfer the dough onto a floured surface and knead it gently until smooth. Roll out the dough to about 1/8 inch (3mm) thickness.

Use a round cutter or a small plate to cut out circles from the dough.

Place a spoonful of the ackee filling onto one half of each dough circle, leaving a small border around the edges.

Fold the other half of the dough over the filling to form a half-circle shape. Press the edges together firmly to seal. You can use a fork to crimp the edges for decoration.

Repeat with the remaining dough and filling.

Place the filled turnovers onto a baking sheet lined with parchment paper.

Preheat your oven to 375°F (190°C). Bake the turnovers for 20-25 minutes, or until golden brown and crispy.

Remove from the oven and let the turnovers cool slightly before serving.

Enjoy your homemade Ackee and Ackee Turnovers as a delicious snack or appetizer, perfect for sharing with friends and family!

Spicy Shrimp Patties

Ingredients:

For the Patties:

- 1 lb (450g) shrimp, peeled, deveined, and finely chopped
- 1 small onion, finely chopped
- 2 cloves garlic, minced
- 1 small bell pepper (any color), finely chopped
- 1 tablespoon finely chopped fresh cilantro
- 1 tablespoon finely chopped fresh parsley
- 1 teaspoon paprika
- 1/2 teaspoon cayenne pepper (adjust to taste)
- Salt and pepper to taste
- 1 egg, beaten
- 1/4 cup breadcrumbs
- 2 tablespoons olive oil, for frying

For Serving (optional):

- Burger buns
- Lettuce
- Tomato slices
- Sliced avocado
- Spicy mayonnaise or aioli

Instructions:

In a large mixing bowl, combine the finely chopped shrimp, finely chopped onion, minced garlic, finely chopped bell pepper, chopped cilantro, chopped parsley, paprika, cayenne pepper, salt, pepper, beaten egg, and breadcrumbs. Mix well until all the ingredients are evenly distributed.

Shape the mixture into patties. If the mixture is too wet to hold its shape, you can add more breadcrumbs as needed.

Heat olive oil in a skillet over medium heat.

Once the oil is hot, add the shrimp patties to the skillet, working in batches if necessary to avoid overcrowding the pan. Cook for about 3-4 minutes on each side, or until golden brown and cooked through. The shrimp should be opaque and firm to the touch.

Once the patties are cooked, remove them from the skillet and place them on a plate lined with paper towels to absorb any excess oil.

Serve the Spicy Shrimp Patties on burger buns with lettuce, tomato slices, sliced avocado, and spicy mayonnaise or aioli if desired.

Enjoy these delicious and flavorful patties as a tasty main dish or sandwich filling!

These Spicy Shrimp Patties are packed with flavor and make for a satisfying meal. They're perfect for a seafood lover's dinner or a summer barbecue. Enjoy!

Jerk Eggplant Turnovers

Ingredients:

For the Filling:

- 1 large eggplant, diced into small cubes
- 1 small onion, finely chopped
- 2 cloves garlic, minced
- 1 tablespoon olive oil
- 2 tablespoons jerk seasoning (adjust to taste)
- Salt and pepper to taste
- 2 tablespoons chopped fresh cilantro or parsley (optional)

For the Dough:

- 2 cups all-purpose flour
- 1/2 teaspoon salt
- 1/2 cup cold butter, cubed
- 1/4 cup cold water

Instructions:

Preheat your oven to 400°F (200°C). Line a baking sheet with parchment paper.
In a large mixing bowl, toss the diced eggplant with olive oil, jerk seasoning, salt, and pepper until evenly coated.
Spread the seasoned eggplant cubes onto the prepared baking sheet in a single layer.
Roast the eggplant in the preheated oven for about 20-25 minutes, or until tender and lightly browned. Remove from the oven and let cool slightly.
In the meantime, prepare the dough. In a large mixing bowl, combine all-purpose flour and salt. Add chilled and cubed butter. Rub the butter into the flour using your fingertips until the mixture resembles coarse crumbs.
Gradually add cold water, a little at a time, and mix until the dough comes together. You may not need to use all the water.
Transfer the dough onto a floured surface and knead it gently until smooth. Roll out the dough to about 1/8 inch (3mm) thickness.

Use a round cutter or a small plate to cut out circles from the dough.

Place a spoonful of the roasted eggplant filling onto one half of each dough circle, leaving a small border around the edges.

Fold the other half of the dough over the filling to form a half-circle shape. Press the edges together firmly to seal. You can use a fork to crimp the edges for decoration.

Repeat with the remaining dough and filling.

Place the filled turnovers onto a baking sheet lined with parchment paper.

Bake the turnovers in the preheated oven for 15-20 minutes, or until golden brown and crispy.

Remove from the oven and let the turnovers cool slightly before serving.

Enjoy your homemade Jerk Eggplant Turnovers as a delicious snack or appetizer!

These Jerk Eggplant Turnovers are bursting with flavor and make for a delightful dish with a Caribbean twist. Serve them as a tasty appetizer or side dish for any occasion!

Corned Beef and Cheese Patties

Ingredients:

For the Patties:

- 1 can (12 oz) corned beef
- 1 cup grated cheddar cheese
- 1 small onion, finely chopped
- 2 cloves garlic, minced
- 1/4 cup breadcrumbs
- 1 egg, beaten
- Salt and pepper to taste
- 2 tablespoons olive oil, for frying

Instructions:

In a large mixing bowl, combine the corned beef, grated cheddar cheese, finely chopped onion, minced garlic, breadcrumbs, beaten egg, salt, and pepper. Mix well until all ingredients are evenly distributed.
Use your hands to shape the mixture into patties of your desired size. If the mixture is too wet to hold its shape, you can add more breadcrumbs as needed.
Heat olive oil in a skillet over medium heat.
Once the oil is hot, add the patties to the skillet, working in batches if necessary to avoid overcrowding the pan. Cook for about 3-4 minutes on each side, or until golden brown and heated through.
Once the patties are cooked, remove them from the skillet and place them on a plate lined with paper towels to absorb any excess oil.
Serve the Corned Beef and Cheese Patties hot, with your favorite dipping sauce or as part of a meal with sides.
Enjoy these flavorful and satisfying patties as a delicious main dish or appetizer!

These Corned Beef and Cheese Patties are easy to make and packed with savory flavor from the corned beef and melted cheese. They're perfect for a quick and tasty meal any time of day!

Coconut Curry Shrimp Turnovers

Ingredients:

For the Filling:

- 1 lb (450g) shrimp, peeled, deveined, and chopped
- 1 small onion, finely chopped
- 2 cloves garlic, minced
- 1 small bell pepper (any color), finely chopped
- 1 tablespoon curry powder
- 1 teaspoon ground turmeric
- 1/2 teaspoon ground cumin
- 1/2 teaspoon ground coriander
- 1/4 teaspoon cayenne pepper (optional, for heat)
- 1 cup coconut milk
- Salt and pepper to taste
- 2 tablespoons olive oil

For the Dough:

- 2 cups all-purpose flour
- 1/2 teaspoon salt
- 1/2 cup cold butter, cubed
- 1/4 cup cold water

Instructions:

In a skillet, heat olive oil over medium heat. Add chopped onion and minced garlic and sauté until softened, about 2-3 minutes.
Add chopped bell pepper to the skillet and cook until softened, about 3-4 minutes.
Stir in curry powder, ground turmeric, ground cumin, ground coriander, and cayenne pepper (if using). Cook for another minute, until fragrant.
Add chopped shrimp to the skillet and cook until they turn pink and opaque, about 3-4 minutes.

Pour in coconut milk and stir until well combined. Let the mixture simmer for 5-7 minutes, until the sauce thickens slightly. Season with salt and pepper to taste. Remove from heat and let the filling cool slightly.

In the meantime, prepare the dough. In a large mixing bowl, combine all-purpose flour and salt. Add chilled and cubed butter. Rub the butter into the flour using your fingertips until the mixture resembles coarse crumbs.

Gradually add cold water, a little at a time, and mix until the dough comes together. You may not need to use all the water.

Transfer the dough onto a floured surface and knead it gently until smooth. Roll out the dough to about 1/8 inch (3mm) thickness.

Use a round cutter or a small plate to cut out circles from the dough.

Place a spoonful of the shrimp filling onto one half of each dough circle, leaving a small border around the edges.

Fold the other half of the dough over the filling to form a half-circle shape. Press the edges together firmly to seal. You can use a fork to crimp the edges for decoration.

Repeat with the remaining dough and filling.

Place the filled turnovers onto a baking sheet lined with parchment paper.

Preheat your oven to 375°F (190°C). Bake the turnovers for 20-25 minutes, or until golden brown and crispy.

Remove from the oven and let the turnovers cool slightly before serving.

Enjoy your homemade Coconut Curry Shrimp Turnovers as a delicious snack or appetizer, packed with flavorful shrimp and aromatic coconut curry sauce!

Callaloo and Sweet Potato Patties

Ingredients:

For the Filling:

- 1 cup callaloo, finely chopped (substitute with spinach if callaloo is not available)
- 1 medium sweet potato, peeled, cooked, and mashed
- 1 small onion, finely chopped
- 2 cloves garlic, minced
- 1 tablespoon olive oil
- 1/2 teaspoon ground cumin
- 1/2 teaspoon ground coriander
- Salt and pepper to taste
- 2 tablespoons chopped fresh cilantro or parsley (optional)

For the Dough:

- 2 cups all-purpose flour
- 1/2 teaspoon salt
- 1/2 cup cold butter, cubed
- 1/4 cup cold water

Instructions:

In a skillet, heat olive oil over medium heat. Add chopped onion and minced garlic and sauté until softened, about 2-3 minutes.

Add chopped callaloo (or spinach) to the skillet and cook until wilted, about 3-4 minutes.

Stir in mashed sweet potato, ground cumin, ground coriander, salt, and pepper. Cook for another 2-3 minutes, stirring occasionally, until the flavors meld together. Remove from heat and let the filling cool slightly.

In the meantime, prepare the dough. In a large mixing bowl, combine all-purpose flour and salt. Add chilled and cubed butter. Rub the butter into the flour using your fingertips until the mixture resembles coarse crumbs.

Gradually add cold water, a little at a time, and mix until the dough comes together. You may not need to use all the water.

Transfer the dough onto a floured surface and knead it gently until smooth. Roll out the dough to about 1/8 inch (3mm) thickness.

Use a round cutter or a small plate to cut out circles from the dough.

Place a spoonful of the callaloo and sweet potato filling onto one half of each dough circle, leaving a small border around the edges.

Fold the other half of the dough over the filling to form a half-circle shape. Press the edges together firmly to seal. You can use a fork to crimp the edges for decoration.

Repeat with the remaining dough and filling.

Place the filled turnovers onto a baking sheet lined with parchment paper.

Preheat your oven to 375°F (190°C). Bake the turnovers for 20-25 minutes, or until golden brown and crispy.

Remove from the oven and let the turnovers cool slightly before serving.

Enjoy your homemade Callaloo and Sweet Potato Patties as a delicious snack or appetizer, perfect for sharing with friends and family!

Curry Beef Turnovers

Ingredients:

For the Filling:

- 1 lb (450g) ground beef
- 1 small onion, finely chopped
- 2 cloves garlic, minced
- 1 small potato, peeled and diced into small cubes
- 1 carrot, peeled and diced into small cubes
- 2 tablespoons curry powder
- 1 teaspoon ground cumin
- 1/2 teaspoon ground turmeric
- 1/2 teaspoon ground coriander
- 1/4 teaspoon cayenne pepper (optional, for heat)
- Salt and pepper to taste
- 2 tablespoons olive oil
- 1/4 cup water
- 2 tablespoons chopped fresh cilantro (optional)

For the Dough:

- 2 cups all-purpose flour
- 1/2 teaspoon salt
- 1/2 cup cold butter, cubed
- 1/4 cup cold water

Instructions:

In a skillet, heat olive oil over medium heat. Add chopped onion and minced garlic and sauté until softened, about 2-3 minutes.
Add ground beef to the skillet and cook until browned, breaking it apart with a spoon as it cooks.
Add diced potato and carrot to the skillet and cook for another 5 minutes, stirring occasionally, until they start to soften.
Stir in curry powder, ground cumin, ground turmeric, ground coriander, cayenne pepper (if using), salt, and pepper. Cook for another minute until fragrant.

Pour in water and let the mixture simmer for 10-15 minutes, or until the vegetables are tender and the flavors meld together. Remove from heat and let the filling cool slightly. Stir in chopped fresh cilantro if using.

In the meantime, prepare the dough. In a large mixing bowl, combine all-purpose flour and salt. Add chilled and cubed butter. Rub the butter into the flour using your fingertips until the mixture resembles coarse crumbs.

Gradually add cold water, a little at a time, and mix until the dough comes together. You may not need to use all the water.

Transfer the dough onto a floured surface and knead it gently until smooth. Roll out the dough to about 1/8 inch (3mm) thickness.

Use a round cutter or a small plate to cut out circles from the dough.

Place a spoonful of the beef filling onto one half of each dough circle, leaving a small border around the edges.

Fold the other half of the dough over the filling to form a half-circle shape. Press the edges together firmly to seal. You can use a fork to crimp the edges for decoration.

Repeat with the remaining dough and filling.

Place the filled turnovers onto a baking sheet lined with parchment paper.

Preheat your oven to 375°F (190°C). Bake the turnovers for 20-25 minutes, or until golden brown and crispy.

Remove from the oven and let the turnovers cool slightly before serving.

Enjoy your homemade Curry Beef Turnovers as a delicious snack or appetizer, packed with flavorful beef and aromatic curry spices!

Jamaican Ackee Patties

Ingredients:

For the Filling:

- 1 can (19 oz) ackee, drained and rinsed
- 1 small onion, finely chopped
- 1 small tomato, diced
- 2 cloves garlic, minced
- 1/2 bell pepper, finely chopped
- 2 sprigs of fresh thyme, leaves only
- 1/2 teaspoon paprika
- 1/2 teaspoon curry powder
- 1/4 teaspoon ground allspice
- Salt and pepper to taste
- 2 tablespoons olive oil

For the Dough:

- 2 cups all-purpose flour
- 1/2 teaspoon salt
- 1/2 cup cold butter, cubed
- 1/4 cup cold water

Instructions:

In a skillet, heat olive oil over medium heat. Add chopped onion, minced garlic, and bell pepper. Sauté until softened, about 3-4 minutes.
Add diced tomato, thyme leaves, paprika, curry powder, and ground allspice to the skillet. Cook for another 2-3 minutes until the tomatoes are softened.
Gently fold in the drained ackee, taking care not to break up the ackee too much. Cook for another 3-4 minutes, stirring occasionally, until heated through. Season with salt and pepper to taste. Remove from heat and let the filling cool slightly.
In the meantime, prepare the dough. In a large mixing bowl, combine all-purpose flour and salt. Add chilled and cubed butter. Rub the butter into the flour using your fingertips until the mixture resembles coarse crumbs.

Gradually add cold water, a little at a time, and mix until the dough comes together. You may not need to use all the water.

Transfer the dough onto a floured surface and knead it gently until smooth. Roll out the dough to about 1/8 inch (3mm) thickness.

Use a round cutter or a small plate to cut out circles from the dough.

Place a spoonful of the ackee filling onto one half of each dough circle, leaving a small border around the edges.

Fold the other half of the dough over the filling to form a half-circle shape. Press the edges together firmly to seal. You can use a fork to crimp the edges for decoration.

Repeat with the remaining dough and filling.

Place the filled turnovers onto a baking sheet lined with parchment paper.

Preheat your oven to 375°F (190°C). Bake the turnovers for 20-25 minutes, or until golden brown and crispy.

Remove from the oven and let the turnovers cool slightly before serving.

Enjoy your homemade Jamaican Ackee Patties as a delicious snack or appetizer,

packed with the unique flavor of ackee and traditional Jamaican spices!

Saltfish and Pumpkin Turnovers

Ingredients:

For the Filling:

- 1 cup salted codfish (saltfish), soaked and flaked
- 1 cup pumpkin puree (canned or homemade)
- 1 small onion, finely chopped
- 2 cloves garlic, minced
- 1/2 teaspoon dried thyme
- 1/4 teaspoon black pepper
- 1/4 teaspoon paprika
- Salt to taste
- 2 tablespoons olive oil

For the Dough:

- 2 cups all-purpose flour
- 1/2 teaspoon salt
- 1/2 cup cold butter, cubed
- 1/4 cup cold water

Instructions:

Preheat your oven to 375°F (190°C). Line a baking sheet with parchment paper.
In a skillet, heat olive oil over medium heat. Add chopped onion and minced garlic and sauté until softened, about 2-3 minutes.
Add flaked saltfish to the skillet and cook for about 5 minutes, stirring occasionally.
Stir in pumpkin puree, dried thyme, black pepper, paprika, and salt to taste. Cook for another 5 minutes, stirring occasionally, until the flavors meld together. Remove from heat and let the filling cool slightly.
In the meantime, prepare the dough. In a large mixing bowl, combine all-purpose flour and salt. Add chilled and cubed butter. Rub the butter into the flour using your fingertips until the mixture resembles coarse crumbs.
Gradually add cold water, a little at a time, and mix until the dough comes together. You may not need to use all the water.

Transfer the dough onto a floured surface and knead it gently until smooth. Roll out the dough to about 1/8 inch (3mm) thickness.

Use a round cutter or a small plate to cut out circles from the dough.

Place a spoonful of the saltfish and pumpkin filling onto one half of each dough circle, leaving a small border around the edges.

Fold the other half of the dough over the filling to form a half-circle shape. Press the edges together firmly to seal. You can use a fork to crimp the edges for decoration.

Repeat with the remaining dough and filling.

Place the filled turnovers onto the prepared baking sheet.

Bake the turnovers in the preheated oven for 20-25 minutes, or until golden brown and crispy.

Remove from the oven and let the turnovers cool slightly before serving.

Enjoy your homemade Saltfish and Pumpkin Turnovers as a delicious snack or appetizer, perfect for sharing with friends and family!

Spicy Lentil Patties

Ingredients:

For the Patties:

- 1 cup dried green or brown lentils
- 2 cups water or vegetable broth
- 1 small onion, finely chopped
- 2 cloves garlic, minced
- 1 small carrot, grated
- 1 teaspoon ground cumin
- 1 teaspoon paprika
- 1/2 teaspoon chili powder (adjust to taste)
- Salt and pepper to taste
- 1/4 cup breadcrumbs
- 1 tablespoon olive oil

For Serving (optional):

- Burger buns or lettuce leaves
- Tomato slices
- Avocado slices
- Spicy mayo or tahini sauce

Instructions:

Rinse the lentils under cold water and drain them. Place them in a medium-sized saucepan with water or vegetable broth. Bring to a boil, then reduce the heat and simmer for 20-25 minutes, or until the lentils are tender and most of the liquid is absorbed. Drain any excess liquid and let the lentils cool slightly.
Preheat your oven to 375°F (190°C). Line a baking sheet with parchment paper.
In a large mixing bowl, mash the cooked lentils with a fork or potato masher until they are mostly mashed but still have some texture.
Add chopped onion, minced garlic, grated carrot, ground cumin, paprika, chili powder, salt, pepper, and breadcrumbs to the mashed lentils. Mix well until all ingredients are combined.
Shape the mixture into patties of your desired size and thickness.

Heat olive oil in a skillet over medium heat. Once the oil is hot, add the lentil patties to the skillet, working in batches if necessary to avoid overcrowding the pan. Cook for about 3-4 minutes on each side, or until golden brown and crispy. Transfer the browned lentil patties to the prepared baking sheet.

Bake the lentil patties in the preheated oven for 10-15 minutes, or until heated through and crispy on the outside.

Serve the Spicy Lentil Patties on burger buns or lettuce leaves, topped with tomato slices, avocado slices, and a drizzle of spicy mayo or tahini sauce if desired.

Enjoy these flavorful and satisfying patties as a delicious vegetarian or vegan main dish!

These Spicy Lentil Patties are packed with protein and flavor, making them a perfect meatless option for any meal. Enjoy!

Jerk Turkey Turnovers

Ingredients:

For the Filling:

- 1 lb ground turkey
- 1 small onion, finely chopped
- 2 cloves garlic, minced
- 1 small bell pepper (any color), finely chopped
- 2 tablespoons jerk seasoning
- 1/2 teaspoon dried thyme
- 1/4 teaspoon black pepper
- Salt to taste
- 2 tablespoons olive oil

For the Dough:

- 2 cups all-purpose flour
- 1/2 teaspoon salt
- 1/2 cup cold butter, cubed
- 1/4 cup cold water

Instructions:

In a skillet, heat olive oil over medium heat. Add chopped onion and minced garlic and sauté until softened, about 2-3 minutes.

Add chopped bell pepper to the skillet and cook until softened, about 3-4 minutes.

Add ground turkey to the skillet and cook until browned, breaking it apart with a spoon as it cooks.

Stir in jerk seasoning, dried thyme, black pepper, and salt to taste. Cook for another 2-3 minutes, until the flavors meld together. Remove from heat and let the filling cool slightly.

In the meantime, prepare the dough. In a large mixing bowl, combine all-purpose flour and salt. Add chilled and cubed butter. Rub the butter into the flour using your fingertips until the mixture resembles coarse crumbs.

Gradually add cold water, a little at a time, and mix until the dough comes together. You may not need to use all the water.

Transfer the dough onto a floured surface and knead it gently until smooth. Roll out the dough to about 1/8 inch (3mm) thickness.

Use a round cutter or a small plate to cut out circles from the dough.

Place a spoonful of the turkey filling onto one half of each dough circle, leaving a small border around the edges.

Fold the other half of the dough over the filling to form a half-circle shape. Press the edges together firmly to seal. You can use a fork to crimp the edges for decoration.

Repeat with the remaining dough and filling.

Place the filled turnovers onto a baking sheet lined with parchment paper.

Preheat your oven to 375°F (190°C). Bake the turnovers for 20-25 minutes, or until golden brown and crispy.

Remove from the oven and let the turnovers cool slightly before serving.

Enjoy your homemade Jerk Turkey Turnovers as a delicious snack or appetizer, packed with flavorful turkey and aromatic jerk seasoning!

Plantain and Black Bean Patties

Ingredients:

For the Patties:

- 2 ripe plantains
- 1 can (15 oz) black beans, drained and rinsed
- 1 small onion, finely chopped
- 2 cloves garlic, minced
- 1 teaspoon ground cumin
- 1 teaspoon paprika
- 1/2 teaspoon chili powder (optional)
- Salt and pepper to taste
- 1/4 cup breadcrumbs
- 2 tablespoons chopped fresh cilantro (optional)
- 2 tablespoons olive oil, for frying

Instructions:

Peel the plantains and cut them into chunks. Place the plantain chunks in a pot of boiling water and cook for about 10-15 minutes, or until softened. Drain and let them cool slightly.

In a large mixing bowl, mash the cooked plantains with a fork until smooth.

Add the drained and rinsed black beans to the mashed plantains and mash them together until well combined, but still leaving some texture.

Add finely chopped onion, minced garlic, ground cumin, paprika, chili powder (if using), salt, pepper, breadcrumbs, and chopped cilantro (if using) to the plantain and black bean mixture. Mix well until all ingredients are evenly distributed.

Shape the mixture into patties of your desired size and thickness.

Heat olive oil in a skillet over medium heat. Once the oil is hot, add the patties to the skillet, working in batches if necessary to avoid overcrowding the pan.

Cook the patties for about 3-4 minutes on each side, or until golden brown and crispy.

Once cooked, remove the patties from the skillet and place them on a plate lined with paper towels to absorb any excess oil.

Serve the Plantain and Black Bean Patties hot, with your favorite dipping sauce or as part of a meal with sides.

Enjoy these flavorful and satisfying patties as a delicious vegetarian or vegan main dish!

These Plantain and Black Bean Patties are packed with flavor from the sweet plantains and hearty black beans. They make a perfect meatless option for any meal!

Callaloo and Sweet Pepper Turnovers

Ingredients:

For the Filling:

- 1 cup callaloo, finely chopped (substitute with spinach if unavailable)
- 1 small red bell pepper, finely chopped
- 1 small yellow bell pepper, finely chopped
- 1 small onion, finely chopped
- 2 cloves garlic, minced
- 1 tablespoon olive oil
- 1/2 teaspoon dried thyme
- Salt and pepper to taste
- 1/4 teaspoon red pepper flakes (optional)
- 1/4 cup coconut milk (optional)

For the Dough:

- 2 cups all-purpose flour
- 1/2 teaspoon salt
- 1/2 cup cold butter, cubed
- 1/4 cup cold water

Instructions:

In a skillet, heat olive oil over medium heat. Add chopped onion and minced garlic and sauté until softened, about 2-3 minutes.

Add chopped bell peppers to the skillet and cook until softened, about 3-4 minutes.

Add chopped callaloo (or spinach) to the skillet and cook until wilted, about 3-4 minutes.

Stir in dried thyme, salt, pepper, and red pepper flakes (if using). Cook for another minute until fragrant. If using coconut milk, add it to the skillet and cook for an additional 2-3 minutes.

Remove from heat and let the filling cool slightly.

In the meantime, prepare the dough. In a large mixing bowl, combine all-purpose flour and salt. Add chilled and cubed butter. Rub the butter into the flour using your fingertips until the mixture resembles coarse crumbs.

Gradually add cold water, a little at a time, and mix until the dough comes together. You may not need to use all the water.

Transfer the dough onto a floured surface and knead it gently until smooth. Roll out the dough to about 1/8 inch (3mm) thickness.

Use a round cutter or a small plate to cut out circles from the dough.

Place a spoonful of the callaloo and sweet pepper filling onto one half of each dough circle, leaving a small border around the edges.

Fold the other half of the dough over the filling to form a half-circle shape. Press the edges together firmly to seal. You can use a fork to crimp the edges for decoration.

Repeat with the remaining dough and filling.

Place the filled turnovers onto a baking sheet lined with parchment paper.

Preheat your oven to 375°F (190°C). Bake the turnovers for 20-25 minutes, or until golden brown and crispy.

Remove from the oven and let the turnovers cool slightly before serving.

Enjoy your homemade Callaloo and Sweet Pepper Turnovers as a delicious snack or appetizer, packed with flavorful vegetables and Caribbean spices!

Vegan Mushroom Patties

Ingredients:

For the Patties:

- 1 lb (450g) mushrooms, finely chopped (you can use a variety such as button, cremini, or portobello)
- 1 small onion, finely chopped
- 2 cloves garlic, minced
- 1 tablespoon olive oil
- 1/2 cup breadcrumbs
- 1/4 cup chopped fresh parsley
- 2 tablespoons nutritional yeast
- 1 tablespoon soy sauce or tamari
- 1 teaspoon dried thyme
- Salt and pepper to taste
- 2 tablespoons ground flaxseeds + 6 tablespoons water (flaxseed egg, optional binder)
- 1/4 cup all-purpose flour (for coating, optional)
- Cooking oil for frying

Instructions:

If using the flaxseed egg as a binder, mix ground flaxseeds and water in a small bowl. Let it sit for about 5 minutes until it thickens.

In a skillet, heat olive oil over medium heat. Add chopped onion and minced garlic and sauté until softened, about 2-3 minutes.

Add chopped mushrooms to the skillet and cook until they release their moisture and begin to brown, about 8-10 minutes.

Stir in soy sauce or tamari, dried thyme, salt, and pepper. Cook for another 2-3 minutes, until any excess moisture evaporates. Remove from heat and let it cool slightly.

In a large mixing bowl, combine the cooked mushroom mixture with breadcrumbs, chopped parsley, nutritional yeast, and flaxseed egg (if using) until well combined.

Shape the mixture into patties of your desired size and thickness.

If using flour for coating, lightly coat each patty in flour.

Heat cooking oil in a skillet over medium-high heat. Once the oil is hot, add the patties to the skillet. Cook for about 4-5 minutes on each side, or until golden brown and crispy.

Once cooked, transfer the patties to a plate lined with paper towels to absorb any excess oil.

Serve the Vegan Mushroom Patties hot, with your favorite dipping sauce or as part of a meal with sides.

Enjoy these flavorful and satisfying patties as a delicious vegan main dish or as a versatile ingredient in sandwiches, wraps, or salads!

Feel free to adjust the seasoning and spices according to your taste preferences. Enjoy your homemade Vegan Mushroom Patties!

Tamarind BBQ Chicken Turnovers

Ingredients:

For the Filling:

- 2 cups cooked shredded chicken (you can use rotisserie chicken or cooked chicken breast)
- 1 small onion, finely chopped
- 2 cloves garlic, minced
- 1/4 cup tamarind paste
- 1/4 cup barbecue sauce
- 1 tablespoon soy sauce or tamari
- 1 tablespoon olive oil
- Salt and pepper to taste
- 1/4 cup chopped fresh cilantro (optional)

For the Dough:

- 2 cups all-purpose flour
- 1/2 teaspoon salt
- 1/2 cup cold butter, cubed
- 1/4 cup cold water

Instructions:

In a skillet, heat olive oil over medium heat. Add chopped onion and minced garlic and sauté until softened, about 2-3 minutes.
Add cooked shredded chicken to the skillet and cook until heated through.
Stir in tamarind paste, barbecue sauce, soy sauce or tamari, salt, and pepper. Cook for another 2-3 minutes until the flavors meld together. Remove from heat and let the filling cool slightly. If using cilantro, stir it in after removing from heat.
In the meantime, prepare the dough. In a large mixing bowl, combine all-purpose flour and salt. Add chilled and cubed butter. Rub the butter into the flour using your fingertips until the mixture resembles coarse crumbs.
Gradually add cold water, a little at a time, and mix until the dough comes together. You may not need to use all the water.

Transfer the dough onto a floured surface and knead it gently until smooth. Roll out the dough to about 1/8 inch (3mm) thickness.

Use a round cutter or a small plate to cut out circles from the dough.

Place a spoonful of the chicken filling onto one half of each dough circle, leaving a small border around the edges.

Fold the other half of the dough over the filling to form a half-circle shape. Press the edges together firmly to seal. You can use a fork to crimp the edges for decoration.

Repeat with the remaining dough and filling.

Place the filled turnovers onto a baking sheet lined with parchment paper.

Preheat your oven to 375°F (190°C). Bake the turnovers for 20-25 minutes, or until golden brown and crispy.

Remove from the oven and let the turnovers cool slightly before serving.

Enjoy your homemade Tamarind BBQ Chicken Turnovers as a delicious snack or appetizer, packed with flavorful chicken and tangy tamarind barbecue sauce!